THE INSANELY E GUIDE TO THE 2021 IPAD PRO (WITH M1 CHIP)

GETTING STARTED WITH THE LATEST GENERATION OF IPAD PRO AND IPADOS 14.5

SCOTT LA COUNTE

ANAHEIM, CALIFORNIA

www.RidiculouslySimpleBooks.com

Copyright © 2021 by Scott La Counte.

All rights reserved. No part of this publication may be reproduced, distributed or transmitted in any form or by any means, including photocopying, recording, or other electronic or mechanical methods, without the prior written permission of the publisher, except in the case of brief quotations embodied in critical reviews and certain other noncommercial uses permitted by copyright law.

Limited Liability / Disclaimer of Warranty. While best efforts have been used in preparing this book, the author and publishers make no representations or warranties of any kind and assume no liabilities of any kind with respect to accuracy or completeness of the content and specifically the author nor publisher shall be held liable or responsible to any person or entity with respect to any loss or incidental or consequential damages caused or alleged to have been caused, directly, or indirectly without limitations, by the information or programs contained herein. Furthermore, readers should be aware that the Internet sites listed in this work may have changed or disappeared. This work is sold with the understanding that the advice inside may not be suitable in every situation.

Trademarks. Where trademarks are used in this book this infers no endorsement or any affiliation with this book. Any trademarks (including, but not limiting to, screenshots) used in this book are solely used for editorial and educational purposes.

Table of Contents

Introduction *10*

Wait! Where's the Home Button?! *12*

   What Isn't In the Box 13

   Let's Get Cosmetic, Shall We? 15

   The Apple Keyboard and Apple Pencil 19

   Let's Talk About Your Face 20

   Feature This… 22

   Thanks for the Nice Gesture, Apple! 27
      Let's Go Home 27
      Multitask 28
      Mission Control…We're Go for Flashlight 29
      Notify Me How to Get Notifications 30
      Searching for Answers 32
      Calling All Widgets 34
      Smart Stacks 35

   The Ridiculously Simple Chapter One Recap 36

iPad Pro vs. iPad vs. Computer *39*
      iPad Pro vs iPad and iPad Air 41

   Should I Buy a Computer or iPad? 42

   Sidecar 43

Starting Up *49*

Setting Up 49

Gestures 50
- Tap 50
- Tap and Hold 51
- Double Tap 51
- Swipe 51
- Drag 52
- Pinch 52
- Rotate and Tilt 52

Did I Really Just Spend 100s of $ for Emojis? 53

Special Characters 54

Using Dictation 54

Number and Symbol Keyboards 54

Emoji Keyboard 55

Multilingual Typing 55

Configuring International Keyboards 56

The Basics 58

Welcome Home 58

The Dock 59

Making Calls 60

There's An App for That 62

Organizing Apps 62

Messaging 65
- Message Tagging 72
- Pinning Messages 74

Notifications 76

Using AirDrop 77

A Little More Than Basic *84*

Mail 84

Surfing the Internet with Safari 85
Set Your Default Email / Web Browser 90

iTunes.. 91

Apple Music 92

Buying Apps 92

Calendar 95
Creating an Appointment... 95

Maps 96
Map Guides 102

Find My 102

Notes 103

Search Text in App 108

Customizing.. *109*

Screen Time... 110

Do Not Disturb Mode 110

Notifications and Widgets 111

General Settings 112

Sounds 113

Customizing Brightness and Wallpaper................... 113

Privacy 114
Compromised Password... 115
Privacy Report 116

Mail, Contacts, Calendars Settings 116

Adding Facebook and Twitter................................ 117

Family Sharing 118
Creating Custom Shortcuts 119
Continuity and Handoff 123

The Camera 124
Taking Photos and Videos 124
Photo Editing 129
Live Photos 131
Photo Albums and Photo Sharing 132
    Photo Captioning 133
    Hide Photos 134

Animoji? 136
How to Add Your Own Animoji 136

Hey, Siri 140

Apple Services 144
    Introduction 144
    ICloud 145
    Apple Music 157
    Apple News 171

Maintain and Protect 185
Security 185
Encryption 186
Keychain 187
iCloud 188
Battery Tips 189
    Disable Notifications 189
    Brightness 190
    Email 190

Location, Location, Lo…Battery Hog 191
Accessorize 191

Appendix A: Accessories *193*

Apple Pencil 193
Scribble for Apple Pencil 195
Using Apple Pencil With the Notes App 196
Apple Pencil Settings 198

Smart Keyboard for iPad Pro 199

Appendix B: Keyboard Shortcuts *201*

Document Shortcuts 202

Appendix C: Welcome to Note Taking 2.0 .... *204*

Why Notes? 204

The Notes Crash Course 205
Views 206
Folders 206
Viewing Attachments 208
Delete Note 210
Creating a Note 210
Lock Note 210
Create a Table 211
Create a Checklist 213
Add a Style 214
Adding Sketches and Images 215
Adding Collaborators 218
Sharing Notes 219
Searching Notes 220
Exporting Notes 220
Pinning Notes 221
Attaching Files 222
Spell Check 223
Font Formatter 224

iPhone Notes 225

Appendix: Shortcut Keys **231**
    General Shortcuts 231
    Edit Shortcuts 231

Index ***233***

About the Author ***236***

Disclaimer: *Please note, while every effort has been made to ensure accuracy, this book is not endorsed by Apple, Inc. and should be considered unofficial.*

INTRODUCTION

When the iPad was released nearly 10 years ago, it was hard to imagine that a thin tablet could be as powerful as a computer. Innovation in technology has made that a reality and with the next generation of iPad Pro with M1 chip, the iPad Pro is suddenly not only on par with most computers—it's faster than most computers! If that wasn't enough for an upgrade, the screen is better, the graphics are better, the camera is better, and you could even argue the wi-fi is better.

But how exactly do you use this fantastically fast beast of a tablet?! Whether you are new to the iPad or upgrading from an earlier device, this book will cover what you need to know to get started.

Some of the many topics covered include:
- What's new in iPadOS
- Multitasking
- Gestures that you should know
- How to use picture-in-picture mode
- Adding widgets to the Home screen
- Using the Apple Pencil (and Scribble)
- Surfing the Internet with Safari

- Using Sidecar
- Using split screen
- Buying, updating, and removing apps
- Using Siri
- Taking, editing, organizing and sharing photos
- Using pre-installed apps like Reminders, Maps, Notes, Calendar
- And much, much more!

Are you ready to start enjoying your new iPad? Then let's get started!

This guide is not endorsed by Apple, Inc., and should be considered unofficial. It is based on the iPad without a Home button (i.e. the iPad Pro and iPad Air).

[1]
Wait! Where's the Home Button?!

> This chapter will cover:
> - What's in (isn't) in the box
> - The iPad's buttons
> - What's Face ID
> - What are the new features to iPadOS 14
> - How to use the iPad Pro when it doesn't have a physical Home button

This book is based on the iPad Pro and iPad Air, so some things I'm talking about may seem a little different. Don't worry! All iPads work essentially the same way. If you aren't interested in what's in the box (below), then just skip it.

What Isn't In the Box

I don't usually cover what's in the box for product guides. It just seems like filler space and the point of this book is to just tell you what you absolutely need to know.

In the case of the iPad, what's in the box isn't as important as what isn't in the box. Sorry for the double negative, but this really is important (Note: this only applies to the iPad Pro models).

What isn't in the box? Two things:
1. Lightning Adapter
2. Headphones

Let's talk about the adapter first because it ties into headphones.

I know, I know, I know—another adapter, right?!

Apple has decided to move away from the Lightning port, which had been the method for charging iPads and iPhones for years, to USB-C.

USB-C sounds like those USB drives but with a C stuck to the end; so, what's the difference? Cosmetically, USB-C is smaller (about half the size) and reversible (meaning there is no right side up when you insert it into your device).

So, Apple is doing all of this because it's smaller? Not quite! USB-C has three big selling points:

It's faster than regular USB (don't worry, there are USB-C flash drives and they can plug right into your iPad with no special adapter).

More power can go through it—enough to charge a laptop (or iPad in this case).

It's universal.

At first glance, it's easy to look at that adapter and see it as a thorn in your side of endless cords but read that last part again: "It's universal." What does that mean? It means one day soon all devices will use USB-C and you can share the cord. So, there will be no more digging in drawers for the right cable.

So yeah, a little annoying that there's another cable, but bear with them because USB-C is really progressing towards a less cord future.

Ok, so the headphones, or lack thereof. What gives?! Apple can literally put a 1-terabyte hard drive into this slim little tablet, but they can't fit in something as simple as a headphone jack?

I can't speak to Apple's design and limits, but the future of Apple devices seems to point to fewer cords and clutter. That means using Bluetooth headphones.

If you still want traditional wired headphones, you have two options:
1. Buy USB-C headphones. They start for less than $10 and will get cheaper as more people adopt USB-C and it becomes standard.
2. Buy an adapter. These are also less than $10.

Let's Get Cosmetic, Shall We?

So, the real elephant in the room with the newest generation iPad Pro is the Home button or lack thereof. In the next chapters, I'll talk about getting set up, so I know this all sounds a little backward, but because so many people are upgrading to the new iPad from an earlier model that had a Home button, it's worth talking about the main things that will be different about it here.

If you have used the iPad before, then I bet you'll spend a good day continuously putting your thumb where the button used to be! Don't worry! You're going to get through it. In fact, after you get used to it not being there, you'll actually start seeing it's more effective without it.

What's more, the missing Home button is becoming a standard feature on iPhones too; so, if you will be upgrading to a Home-less iPhone soon, then you'll be ready for it because it essentially works the same way on the iPad.

Before diving into the gestures, let's cover some other things that look different about this iPad Pro.

The top portion of the iPad Pro looks like a black bar, right? Look closer. A little more. More. See it? There are cameras there. They kind of camouflage into the black, right? It's just the old-fashioned front-facing selfie camera, right? Yes, but there's more. There's a Dot projector, infrared camera, flood illuminator. They all sound fancy, don't they? Fancy is...well fancy! But what on Earth does that mean in simple terms? It means that the front-facing 7MP camera can take pretty impressive selfies! But all those things also give you what you need for Face ID (which lets you unlock the iPad without the finger sensor you had on previous devices).

Okay, so all that's interesting, right? But you don't actually do anything with the sensors. What about the buttons on the tablet itself? Good question! Thanks for asking!

The button placement isn't too far off from previous iPads.

In the upper right corner, you have three things of note:

1. The front-facing camera (12MP)
2. The Top Button (which powers your device on and off, and puts it in standby)
3. The volume button

Turn the device over and on the right (right assuming the device is turned around) and you have a few more things of note:

4. The back camera (12MP)
5. Flash
6. Smart Connector (this is how the Apple Keyboard, which is sold separately, connects to the iPad)
7. USB-C (where you charge the iPad)
8. SIM Tray (you will only have this if your iPad has cellular)
9. Magnetic connector (this is where you connect the Apple Pencil, sold separately)

The appropriately named "Top Button" is more than a power button. Maybe that's why it's not called the Power button? Hmm. So, what is it?

The Top Button is the button you use to power the iPad on and off—or to put it in standby (which is the mode you put it in after you finish playing Angry Birds in the bathroom and need to set the tablet down for a minute to wash your hands).

The most common use for the Top Button is to wake up your tablet. Picking up your iPad Pro and staring at it with an annoyed or confused expression will also do this. But if you ever find yourself stuck and picking up the tablet isn't waking it up, then just push down on the Top Button and you should be just fine. You can also tap the screen to wake it up.

If you are still on the fence about the iPad Pro and are reading this book just to learn more about it, then it's worth mentioning the actual feel of the device—or rather showing you a few pictures.

The most important picture is the one of the back camera. Take a look at it below. See how it pops out?

Why does that matter? To me it doesn't. But if you are an artist using the device on a flat surface, it's going to give it an unevenness. This can be solved by putting it in a case.

The Apple Keyboard and Apple Pencil

You may have bought the iPad Pro but haven't made your mind up about the Keyboard and Pencil. So, let's talk about both of those things briefly.

The Keyboard is, well, a keyboard! But if you've had the old Apple Keyboard case, then one thing you'll probably be happy about is that old origami style is gone; maybe it's just me, but I always had a hard time figuring out how to fold it! This one is much simpler.

Simpler means one position is gone; on the previous version, it could be used as a stand without the Keyboard. Not the case anymore. It, of course, stands up with the Keyboard open.

It also has two positions, so you can have two viewing angles; this is helpful when you are typing on your lap, but not as functional as the keyboard case with more limitless possibilities with the position.

It's not terribly heavy, but it does add some weight; I recommend testing it at a store before buying.

Next, the Apple Pencil; I'll cover this more later in the book, but I do want to point out that the Pencil is pretty basic for this generation. It's completely redesigned, and it no longer comes with "tips." You have to buy those extra. They're pretty cheap though.

The biggest advantage of the new Apple Pencil is you don't have to plug it in. The previous generation had to be charged at the bottom of the iPad in the charging port, which really could get in the way. This generation is all magnetic.

Let's Talk About Your Face

Things were going okay with you and the Home button. You could rub your thumb over it and like a genie in a bottle, it would magically read your DNA and turn on. Why'd Apple have to go a ruin a good thing?

Sure, getting rid of the button gives you more screen real estate, but plenty of other tablets have added a button to the back of the device so you can have the best of both worlds. It's like Apple is trying to force you to love it, isn't it? I don't know why Apple does everything, but if past history teaches us anything, we have learned that Apple makes us adapt to better things by taking away the things we love. We loved our CD drives...and Apple took them out and put USB drives in their place; we got through it though, didn't we?! They did it again with the headphone jack. And on the iPad Pro and new MacBook's, USB is gone and, in its place, the faster USB-C.

Change is never fun, but it's not necessarily a bad thing. If you like numbers, you'll love this one. That little finger scanner has a ratio of 50,000:1—that's the ratio of how hard it would be for someone to break into your iPad. The iPad Pro with Face ID? 1,000,000:1. So if you're a fan of security, then Face ID is a no brainer.

If you're that person who is always throwing "What if" into the equation (you're the same person who morbidly asked, "What if someone stole my tablet and cut off my finger to unlock it? Would the fingerprint scanner still work?"), then I'm sure you have a few questions. Like:

What if I wear glasses and then take them off or put in contacts?

What if I have a beard and shave it?

What if I think I look like Brad Pitt, but the iPad Pro says I'm more of a Lyle Lovett?

Sorry, Lyle, not everyone can be a Brad—but you don't have to worry about those first two points. Face ID has adaptive recognition, so you'll be just fine if you decide to grow it out for Movember.

If you're in a dark room, Face ID will also still work—albeit with a little bit of help from the light sensor—which is a little annoying if you're lying in bed and the only way to unlock your iPad Pro is to have a light turn on to scan your face. It should be noted, however, that it is pretty good at scanning faces in dark settings. If you're in a dark room, you can also just press that side button to open it manually and skip Face ID.

Feature This…

iPadOS 14 is the latest operating system available for Apple iPad. While iPadOS 14 is free, it is not available to all devices; if you have an older iPad, then it may be time to upgrade to get all the best new features. The following devices are compatible, as of this writing:

- iPad Pro 12.9-inch (4th generation)
- iPad Pro 11-inch (2nd generation)
- iPad Pro 12.9-inch (3rd generation)
- iPad Pro 11-inch (1st generation)
- iPad Pro 12.9-inch (2nd generation)
- iPad Pro 12.9-inch (1st generation)
- iPad Pro 10.5-inch
- iPad Pro 9.7-inch
- iPad (8th generation)
- iPad (7th generation)
- iPad (6th generation)

- iPad (5th generation)
- iPad mini (5th generation)
- iPad mini 4
- iPad Air (4th generation)
- iPad Air (3rd generation)
- iPad Air 2

It should also be noted that not all features are available on older models. So if you hear someone talking about a great new feature on their iPad, and you don't see it, then it's probably because you have an older iPad. Some features also require an Apple Pencil, which costs extra and isn't available on all models.

If you aren't sure what model number you have, go to the Settings app, then tap the General option, and tap About. This will tell you your model name (i.e. iPad Pro) and the model number and serial number. The model number will indicate things like how large the hard drive is; the serial number is likely only something you would need if you are getting your iPad repaired.

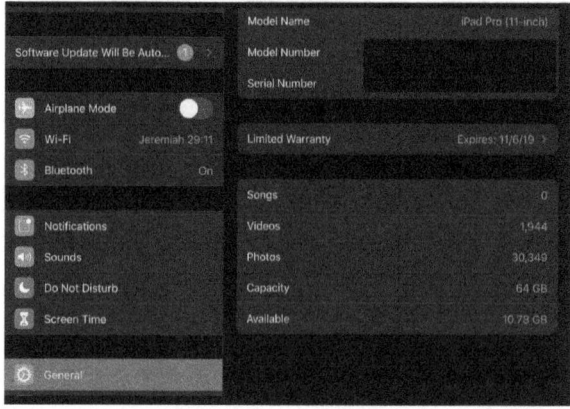

To install iPadOS from a later device, go to Settings > General > Software Update.

Okay, so what are the features?

In terms of the overall look of iPadOS 14, there are two big changes: redesigned Widgets on your Home Screen and a new Scribble feature for Apple Pencil. Both will be covered in greater scope later in this book.

In terms of new features, the biggest ones you should be aware of are below:

- **Scribble** - One of the best features of iPadOS 14 is Scribble...unfortunately, it requires an iPad that's compatible with Apple Pencil and an Apple Pencil. Scribble converts your handwriting into text. So you can write in text fields without having to type. It also supports different gestures; for example, if you make a mistake you can just cross it out to erase it or if you circle a word you can select it and move it. You can also create different shapes, like stars, which are recognized and turned into the shape. Scribble really shines in the Notes app. You can handwrite all of your notes and then convert them into text and paste them into another app (like Pages or Word).

- **Widgets** - If you have ever used Android, you might already know a thing or two about widgets; they've been available to some degree on the iPad for a while, but iPadOS 14 has reimagined them and made them easier to find and use. What are they? Think of them like tiny versions of your app to give you insights without having to open the app—to see the weather, for example, or what calendar events you have coming up.
- **No App Library** – Okay, so this isn't a feature (rather a lack of a feature) but I'm mentioning it here because you might go crazy trying to find it! App Library is a new view on iPhone meant to keep you even more productive and organized. It puts all of your apps in one place and makes it easier to find the apps you commonly use, or search for the ones that you don't. You no longer have to have all of your apps on Home screens; you can hide them in the App Library while keeping them on your phone. Makes sense for

this to be on the iPad, right? But it's not! My guess is it will come with a later update, so stay tuned.
- Translate - Translate is a new Apple app that lets you translate a conversation in real-time; it's great for traveling to other countries. Just say in English what you need to ask and pick the language—or have the person speak into your iPad and it auto detects the language that they are speaking.
- Maps - Maps gets a minor update with iPadOS 14; in addition to all the different types of directions that you can get (like walking, driving and transit), you can now get cycling directions. The app can also give you electric vehicle routing to help you find the best directions that include charging locations.
- Redesigned Messages - Messages comes with several new features; the best: pinning conversations, so you can keep the people you talk to most up high; the reply to mention someone in a group reply, and reply directly to specific messages within a text exchange.
- New Memoji Styles - Memoji works the same as always, but there are more options to dress your avatar up.
- Password Monitoring - Password monitoring alerts you when there's a data

breach somewhere that you have a password stored, so you can change it right away and prevent identity theft.
- Compact Calls - One of the best features in iPadOS 14 is not so much what it does, but how it does it; you'll notice that things like Siri and incoming phone calls are now much more compacted—so you can keep doing what you're doing, and not be pulled away from the app to decline the call.

I'll talk about each of these features later in this book, so don't worry if you don't quite understand them.

If you want the big giant list of everything new in iPadOS 14, visit: https://www.apple.com/ipados/features/

THANKS FOR THE NICE GESTURE, APPLE!

And now the moment you've been reading for: how to make your way around an iPad Pro without the Home button.

Remember, these gestures are pretty universal—they work on the iPad Pro and they work on iPhones that don't have the Home button.

LET'S GO HOME

First, the easiest gesture: getting to your Home screen. Do you have your pen and paper ready? It's complicated...swipe up from the bottom of your screen.

That's it.

It's not too far off from pushing a button. Heck, your finger's even in the same place! The only difference is you're moving your thumb upward instead of inward.

Multitask

As Dorothy would say, there's no place like Home—but we can still give a shout out to multitask, can't we? If you don't know what it is, multitask is how you switch quickly between apps—you're in iMessage and want to open up Safari to get a website, for example; instead of closing iMessage, finding Safari from the Home screen, and then repeating the process to get back, you use multitask to do it quickly.

On the old iPad's you would double press the Home button. On the new iPad Pro, you Swipe Up from the bottom as if you were going to Home...but don't lift your finger; instead of lifting your finger, continue swiping up until you reach the middle of your screen—at this point, you should see the multitask interface.

If you have an app open (Note: this does not work on the Home screen), you can also slide your finger right across the bottom edge of the screen; this will go to the previous app open.

Mission Control...We're Go for Flashlight

If you haven't noticed, I'm putting these features in order of use. So, the third most common gesture people use is the Control Center. That's where all your Controls are located—go figure...Control is where controls are!

We'll go over the Control Center in more detail later in the book. For now, just know that this is where you'll do things like adjust brightness, enable airplane mode, and turn on the beloved flashlight. On the old iPad, you accessed Control Center by swiping up from the bottom of the screen. No Bueno on the new iPad Pro—if you recall, swiping up gets you Home.

The new gesture for Control Center is swiping down from the upper right corner of the iPad Pro (not the top middle, which will do something else).

Notify Me How to Get Notifications

Eck! So many gestures to remember! Let me throw you a bone. To see notifications (those are the alerts like email and text that you get on your tablet and phone), swipe down from the middle of the screen. That's the same way you did it before! Finally, nothing new to remember!

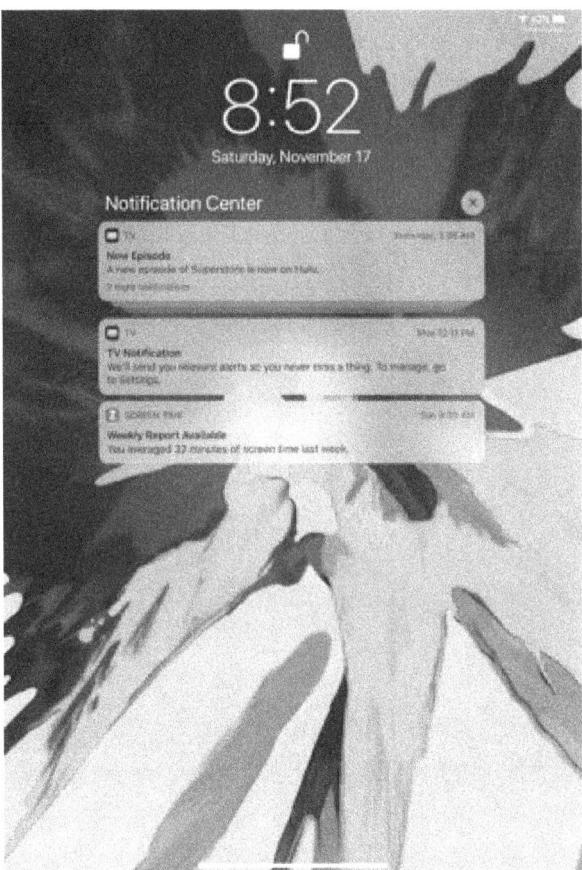

I hate to steal your bone back, but about not remembering anything new: there is something to remember. :-(

If you swipe down from the right corner, you get the Control Center; that wasn't the case on old iPads. Swiping down anywhere on top got you to the Home screen. On the new iPad Pro, you can only swipe in the middle.

SEARCHING FOR ANSWERS

If you're like me, you probably have a million apps—and because you want to see the wallpaper on your iPad Pro's Home screen, you put those million apps in one folder! That may not be the best way to organize a library, but the search function on the iPad Pro, makes it easy to find anything quickly.

In addition to apps, you can use search to find calendar dates, contacts, things on the Internet. The best part of search? Works the same way it does on older iPads...there's your bone back! From your Home screen, swipe down in the middle of the screen.

CALLING ALL WIDGETS

Many apps come with what's known as a Widget. Widgets are basically mini versions of your favorite app—so you can see the weather, for example, without actually opening the app.

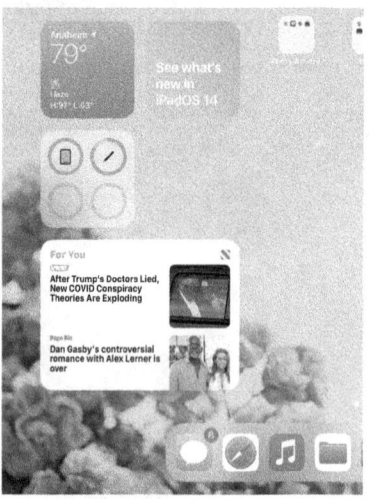

The gesture to see widgets is the same on the new iPad Pro as the old. Hurray! Something else you don't have to learn. From the Home or Lock screen, swipe right and they'll come out.

This is a little different from what you might be used to on an iPhone. Unlike the iPhone, you can't put Widgets on the wallpaper—they just sit on the right side, so you have to swipe to see them.

Smart Stacks

You can also add what's known as a Smart Stack as a widget. This is a widget that changes based on what it predicts you will use during one point in the day.

If the widget is the same size, you can drag it into another widget box to create your own Smart Stack.

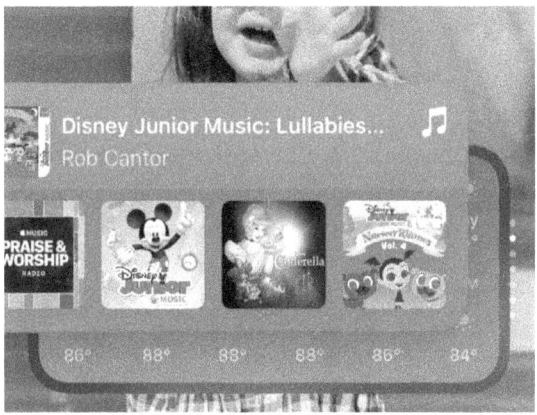

Once added, you can swipe up and down within that widget to toggle between the app.

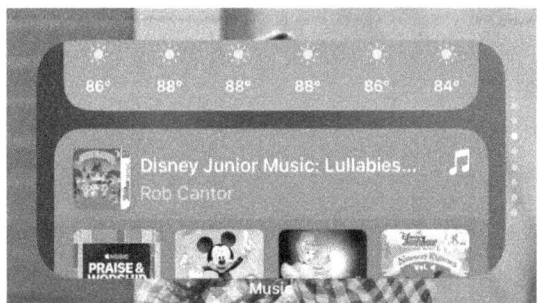

If you long-press on it, you are able to edit the stack.

When you edit it, you can move what's in the stack and turn off Smart Rotate, so it doesn't rotate throughout the day.

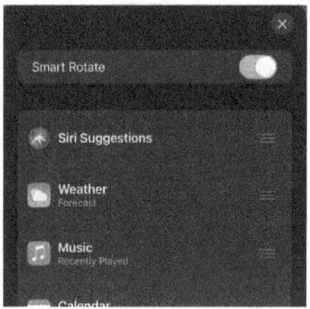

The Ridiculously Simple Chapter One Recap

Okay, so you only got a minute to get up and running, and you need the 1-minute summary of everything important?

Let's cover gestures. The left side will be the way the gesture used to work, and right side will be the way it works on new iPad Pros.

Previous Generation iPad Pro	*Next Generation iPad Pro*
Go to the Home screen - Press the Home button.	Go to the Home screen - Swipe up from the bottom of your screen.
Multitask - Double press Home button.	Multitask - Swipe up from the bottom of your screen, but don't lift your finger until it reaches the middle of the screen.
Control Center - Swipe up from the bottom of the screen.	Control Center - Swipe down from the upper right corner of the iPad Pro.
Notifications - Swipe down from the top of the screen.	Notifications - Swipe down from the middle top of the screen.
Search - From the Home screen, swipe down from the middle of your screen.	Search - From the Home screen, swipe down from the middle of your screen.
Access Widgets - From the Home or Lock screen, swipe right.	Access Widgets - From the Home or Lock screen, swipe right.

[2]
iPad Pro vs. iPad vs. Computer

This chapter will cover:
- What's so special about each models and do you need it?
- Do you still need a computer?
- Sidecar

It seems like every year a new iPad is released, but on the surface they don't always look different. Comparing the 2021 iPad Pro to the previous model is challenging if you are looking at the two side-by-side because they look almost identical. It's really the inside that counts when it comes to comparing the new iPad Pro with previous generations.

Let's start with the chip. A lot has been said about the M1 chip, but what is it and why does it matter? To simplify the chip, what you need to know is it's smaller, and yet more powerful, than most computer chips on the market. Next to the previous iPad, the M1 is said to be about two times faster than the previous generation iPad.

The 2021 iPad Pro also has more memory—which makes multitasking faster. The earlier iPad had 6GB of RAM; the new one starts at 8GB of RAM.

The 2021 iPad Pro also supports thunderbolt cables, which makes transferring large files faster and showing on compatible HD displays sharper.

The new iPad Pro will have models that support 5G—the earlier model only supported 4G.

Looking beyond the speed of the iPad, the next standout feature for a lot of people will be the camera. Apple knows more and more people are working from home and they improved the front-facing camera as a result. It has gone from 7MP on the earlier model to 12MP; Apple has also added a new feature called "Center Stage auto tracking"; this makes the front facing camera automatically move if you are moving—it's great for Zoom calls and tutorials.

Finally there's the new XDR display that's sharper than ever—you'll be blown away by how good some movies and games look!

IPAD PRO VS IPAD AND IPAD AIR

As you probably know, iPad Pro is the most expensive iPad, but not the only one that Apple sells. There are several. The 2020 iPad and iPad Air are the latest generation iPads next to the Pro. How does it stack up against them? And is it really worth paying extra?

When it comes to paying more for the iPad Pro, it really comes down to whether you need better performance. If you are a casual user—meaning you just check email and Facebook, and maybe watch a video or two, then the other iPads are probably perfectly fine for you. You don't need all that extra chip speed to surf the Internet.

If you're the type that loves taking videos and photos on a large tablet, then the Pro has the best camera, but the iPad Air has a pretty sharp one as well—and the iPad's, while not amazing, is still pretty good.

If you are a storage hog, then the iPad Pro is also your best bet because it can be customized all the way to 2TB of storage; the iPad Air tops out at 256GB and the iPad at 128GB.

One last thing you should think about when you consider which iPad is buttons—the iPad Pro and iPad Air don't have a Home button; the iPad does.

Should I Buy a Computer or iPad?

Can an iPad really replace a computer? That really depends. An iPad mini and iPad are ideally more casual products—perfect for when you just want to browse the Internet or check email in bed or on the couch. That isn't to say they can't replace your computer, however—it just depends on what you do on your computer. The iPad Air and Pro is the first Apple tablet that really stands a chance of replacing your computer.

In terms of Apple products (not counting Apple's desktop line: Mac mini, iMac, and Mac Pro), there's basically four products to consider: iPad Pro, MacBook Air, MacBook, and MacBook Pro. Let's look at who is best for each one:

iPad Air and Pro: Great for students, artists, and commuters who want a lightweight tablet with computer-like speeds. For some users, the advantage will also be it's almost the same operating system as the iPhone, so if you know your way around an iPhone, then this will be easy for you.

MacBook Air: The MacBook Air is a terrific lightweight alternative; the biggest trade-off with the MacBook Air used to be graphics, but the latest model fixed this with Retina displays.

MacBook: MacBook was updated in 2015; it looks great—but looks can be deceiving. As it has been pointed out, the iPad Pro (which is cheaper) has outperformed some models in many tests. It's great for portability but is lacking if you have heavy tasks you need to do.

MacBook Pro: The MacBook Pro is Apple's best laptop; it's fast, and still relatively light. It's the best laptop you can buy, but if you aren't using graphic intensive programs, then you probably don't need the best.

Can the iPad replace a computer? For some people, yes. But you'll want to make sure you load up on the right accessories (like a comfortable keyboard), which can make the iPad less portable and even as heavy as a laptop.

Sidecar

There is one more option to consider: get a Mac / MacBook and iPad because they work great together thanks to Sidecar.

What's Sidecar? It's basically using your iPad as a second screen alongside your Mac.

Using your iPad as a second Mac screen is nothing new. Popular apps such as Duet have been doing this successfully for years.

Apple has finally taken note and decide to release a feature called Sidecar that lets you wirelessly use your iPad as a secondary Mac screen; it's just like using AirPlay on your phone to show YouTube on your TV. So long apps like Duet, right? Not exactly.

Before moving into how to use Sidecar, let me first mention what Sidecar is not: a rich app full of pro features. It does one thing very well: shows your Mac screen on your iPad. Apps like Duet are compatible with iPhone and iPad and also work with cross OSes—so you can also show your Windows device on your iPad. But personally, one thing I find lacking on Sidecar is touch. I expected to be able to tap the iPad screen and launch apps and folders. That wasn't the case. It was for display purposes only…unless you have an Apple Pencil. Sidecar feels like it was made to entice people to buy an Apple Pencil. With an Apple Pencil, touch suddenly becomes possible. There's probably a good reason for this—the Apple Pencil is more precise and has more gestures than your finger.

So now that you know a little about what it isn't, let's look at how it works.

First, make sure your MacBook (yes, this is only compatible with MacBooks—sorry Windows users) is up-to-date with the latest OS (Catalina).

Second, make sure your iPad is turned on, in standby mode, and on the same Wi-Fi network (if not, you won't see the next step).

Third, go to the menu in the upper right side of your MacBook and click the rectangular box for AirPlay.

That's it! Kind of. Your MacBook should now be showing on your iPad. It will look a little like this:

So what do I mean "kind of"? There are still a few more settings you should know about. Click that AirPlay box in the right corner again and you'll see even more options.

```
          ▢  ✻  ⌃  ▲  ◀  75% ■
          AirPlay: Looking for TV...
          Disconnect

          AirPlay: Sidecar Display
          ✓ Mirror Built-in Retina Display
          Mirror Sidecar Display
          Use As Separate Display

          Connect to:
          ✓ Scott's iPad (2)

          Scott's iPad (2):
          Hide Sidebar
          Hide Touch Bar

          Open Displays Preferences...
          Open Sidecar Preferences...
```

What are all these options? Use As Separate Display (vs the two Mirror options) turns your iPad into a second screen—so you can have another Mac app running on your display instead of just showing whatever is on your MacBook. The two Hide options get rid of the boxes you see on your iPad to make it a bit more full screen.

Finally, Open Sidecar Preferences will give you a few additional options. You can, for example, pick to show the menu bar on the right instead of left.

You can disconnect from Sidecar by either tapping on the box with the line through it on your iPad or going to the AirPlay button on your Mac and disconnecting.

If you aren't seeing your iPad on your Mac, there's a good chance the reason is your Mac is using a different Apple ID; as I have said, there's limitations to Sidecar and this is yet another—you can't use it on a Mac with a separate ID like you might connecting to an Apple TV.

[3]

Starting Up

This chapter will cover:
- Setup
- Common gestures and terminology
- The keyboard

Setting Up

I don't want to take away from the main topics to spend several pages setting up your iPad Pro. The setup is straightforward, and the onscreen help gives you everything you need to know. There are a few things, however, you should know about the setup:

You can change things. If you say yes (or no) to something but change your mind, you'll be able to change it in the Settings, which I will walk you through in corresponding sections throughout this book.

If you are moving from an older iPad to the iPad Pro and want to keep all of the settings, make sure to back it up before restoring it over the Cloud. To do this, go into Settings. Next, click your account name (first thing you'll see on top). Then iCloud and iCloud Backup (near the middle when you scroll), and finally Back Up Now.

Face ID - Face ID is probably new to you unless you have last year's iPhone X. One thing that's worth pointing out is you can add multiple faces. For example, if your spouse or child uses your tablet, they can add their face to Face ID and won't have to put in a passcode or ask you to unlock it every time they want to use it.

While the iPad Pro box does not contain a manual, there is a manual available online. You can access it here: https://support.apple.com/manuals/ipad

Gestures

Throughout the book, I'll refer to certain gestures. To make sure you understand the terminology, below are the most common ones:

Tap

This is the "click" of the iPad world. A tap is just a brief touch. It doesn't have to be hard or last very long. You'll tap icons, hyperlinks, form choices, and more. You'll also tap numbers on a touch keypad in order to make calls. It's not exactly rocket science, is it!

Tap and Hold

This simply means touching the screen and leaving your finger in contact with the glass. It's useful for bringing up context menus or other options in some apps.

Double Tap

This refers to two rapid taps, like double clicking with your finger. Double tapping will perform different functions in different apps. It will also zoom in on pictures or webpages.

Swipe

Swiping means putting your finger on the surface of your screen and dragging it to a certain point and then removing your finger from the surface. You'll use this motion to navigate through menu levels in your apps, through pages in Safari, and more. It'll become second nature overnight, I promise.

Drag

This is mechanically the same as swiping, but with a different purpose. You'll touch an object to select it, and then drag it to wherever it needs to go and release it. It's just like dragging and dropping with a mouse, but it skips the middleman.

Pinch

Take two fingers, place them on the iPad Pro screen, and move them either toward each other or away from each other in a pinching or reverse pinching motion. Moving your fingers together will zoom in inside many apps, including web browsers and photo viewers; moving them apart will zoom out.

Rotate and Tilt

Many apps on iPad Pro take advantage of rotating and tilting the device itself. For instance, in the paid app Star Walk, you can tilt the screen so that it's pointed at whatever section of the night sky you're interested in—Star Walk will reveal the constellations based on the direction the iPad Pro is pointed.

Did I Really Just Spend 100s of $ for Emojis?

The reason you shelled out $100s for an iPad Pro that's more powerful than many computers was to send out adorable emojis in your text messages, right? Okay…maybe not! But the keyboard, and by extension emojis, is something you use a lot with your iPad, so it's worth learning more about it before digging deeper into the software that relies on them.

Anytime you type a message, the keyboard pops up automatically. There are no extra steps. But there are some things you can do with the keyboard to make it more personal.

There are a few things to notice on the keyboard—the delete key is marked with a little 'x' (it's right next to the letter M), and the shift key is the key with the upward arrow (next to the letter Z).

By default, the first letter you type will be capitalized. You can tell what case the letters are in though at a quick glance.

To use the shift key, just tap it and then tap the letter you want to capitalize or the alternate punctuation you'd like to use. Alternatively, you can touch the shift key and drag your finger to the letter you want to capitalize. Double tap the shift key to enter caps lock (i.e. everything is capitalized) and tap once to exit caps lock.

Special Characters

To type special characters, just tap and hold the key of the associated letter until options pop up. Drag your finger to the character you want to use and be on your way. What exactly would you use this for? Let's say you're are writing something in Spanish and need the accent on the "e"; tapping and holding on the "e" will bring that option up.

Using Dictation

Let's face it: typing on the keyboard stinks sometimes! Wouldn't be easier to just say what you want to write? If that sounds like you, then Dictation can help! Just tap the microphone next to the spacebar and start talking. It works pretty well.

Number and Symbol Keyboards

Of course, there's more to life than letters and exclamation points. If you need to use numbers, tap the 123 key in the bottom left corner. This will bring up a different keyboard with numbers and punctuation.

From this keyboard, you can get back to the alphabet by tapping the ABC key in the bottom left corner. You can also access an additional keyboard which includes the remaining standard symbols by tapping the #+- key, just above the ABC key.

Emoji Keyboard

And finally, the moment you've waited for! Emojis!

The emoji keyboard is accessible using the smiley face key between the 123 key and the dictation key. Emojis are tiny cartoon images that you can use to liven up your text messages or other written output. This goes far beyond the colon-based emoticons of yesteryear—there are enough emojis on your iPad Pro to create an entire visual vocabulary.

To use the emoji keyboard, note that there are categories along the bottom (and that the globe icon on the far left will return you to the world of language). Within those categories, there are several screens of pictographs to choose from. Many of the human emojis include multicultural variations. Just press and hold them to reveal other options.

Multilingual Typing

Most people are probably all set. They know all they need to know about typing on the iPad and they're ready to blast emojis at their friends. There are a few other features that apply to some (not all people)

One such feature is Multilingual Typing. This is for people who type multiple languages at the same time. So, if you type between Spanish and English, you won't keep seeing a message saying your spelling is wrong.

If that sounds like you, then you just need to enable another dictionary, which is simple. Go to Settings > General > Dictionary.

Configuring International Keyboards

If you find yourself typing in a different language fairly often, you may want to set up international keyboards. To set up international keyboards, visit Settings > General > Keyboard > Keyboards. You can then add an appropriate international keyboard by tapping Add New Keyboard. As an example, iPad Pro has great support for Chinese text entry—choose from pinyin, stroke, zhuyin, and handwriting, where you actually sketch out the character yourself.

When you enable another keyboard, the smiley emoji key will change to a globe icon. To use international keyboards, tap the globe key to cycle through your keyboard choices.

Your iPad Pro is loaded with features to help prevent slip-ups, including Apple's battle-tested autocorrect feature, which guards against common typos. In iOS 8, Apple introduced a predictive text feature that predicts what words you're most likely to type, and its accuracy is even better in the new iPadOS.

Three choices appear just above the keyboard—the entry as typed, plus two best guesses. Predictive text is somewhat context-specific, too. It learns your speech patterns as you email your boss or text your best friend, and it will serve up appropriate suggestions based on who you're messaging or emailing. Of course, if it bothers you, you can turn it off by visiting Settings > General > Keyboards and turning off predictive text by sliding the green slider to the left.

[4]
THE BASICS

This chapter will cover:
- Home screen
- Making calls
- Adding and removing apps
- Sending messages
- iMessage apps
- Notifications
- AirDrop
- Multitasking

WELCOME HOME

There's one thing that has pretty much stayed the same since the very first iPad was released: The Home screen. The look has evolved (and the dock on the bottom has changed a little), but the layout has not. All you need to know about it is it's the main screen. So, when you read me say "go to the Home screen" this is the screen I'm talking about. Make sense?

THE DOCK

The dock is the bottom portion of your Home screen.

This is where you can "dock" the apps you love and use the most. If you've used an older iPad or iPhone, then I'm sure you know all about it. But this dock is a little different.

Look at the above screenshot. Now look to the right. See that line? If not, look at the one below:

The apps to the right of that line are not put there by you. These are the last three apps you've used. So, these will always be changing. It helps you multitask much quicker.

MAKING CALLS

Your iPad Pro is a great phone.

You read that right! In addition to thousands of other things, your iPad Pro can make phone calls. It does this two ways:

Over Wi-Fi with FaceTime Audio
With your iPhone

There are a number of ways you can make calls:

- If you are on a website or map and there's a phone number with a hyperlink, that means you can tap it and it will dial

the number. Note: to do this, you have to have an iPhone tethered to your iPad Pro. The call will come from your iPhone's phone number.
- If someone sends you an iMessage on your iPad (we'll cover iMessage later in this chapter), you can tap that name and tap FaceTime Audio; the call will be made using FaceTime Audio.

info@orders.apple.com

audio   FaceTime   info

- The Contacts app has a list of all your contacts (hence the app's name!); any contact who has an iPhone that's tied to the given email will have a FaceTime Audio option—or, if your iPhone is tethered to your iPad Pro, an option to dial them directly.

Receiving a call is fairly intuitive. If your iPad Pro is tied to your iPhone, and the phone is in range of the iPad Pro, then the call will come to your iPad Pro as well. Swipe to answer. That's it.

There's An App for That

App is short for application. So, when you hear the term "There's an app for that," it just means there's a program that does what you want to do. If you're a Windows user, all those things you always open (like Word and Excel) are apps. Apple has literally millions of apps. Opening an app is as simple as touching it.

Unlike apps on a computer, you don't have to close apps on your iPad. It's all automatic. For most apps, it will even remember where you were so when you open it again, it's saved.

Organizing Apps

If you're like me—and pretty much most people are—you love your apps and you have a lot of them! So, you'll need to know how to move them around, put them in folders, and delete them. It's all easy to do.

The Home screen may be the first screen you see, but if you swipe to the right, you'll see there are more. Personally, I keep the most used apps on the first screen, and not-so-used apps in folders on the second. The bottom dock is where I put the apps I use all the time (like Mail and Safari).

To rearrange apps, take your finger and touch one of your apps and hold it there until the icon jiggles. When the apps are jiggling like that, you can touch them without opening them and drag them around your screen. Try it out! Just touch an app and drag your finger to move it. When you've found the perfect spot, lift your finger and the app drops into place. After you've downloaded more apps, you can also drag apps across Home screens.

You can delete an app using the same method for moving them. The only difference is instead of moving them, you tap the 'x' in the upper left corner of the icon. Don't worry about deleting something on accident. Apps are stored in the Cloud. You can delete and install them as many times as you want; you don't have to pay again—you just have to download them again.

Putting apps on different screens is helpful, but to be really organized you want to use folders. You can, for example, have a folder for all your game apps, finance apps, social apps, whatever you want. You pick what to name it. If you want an "Apps I use on the toilet" folder, then you can absolutely have it!

To create a folder, just drag one app over another app you'd like to add into that folder.

Once they are together, you can name the folder. To delete the folder, just put the folder apps in "jiggle mode" and drag them out of the folder. iPad Pro doesn't allow empty folders—when a folder is empty, iPad Pro deletes it automatically.

Messaging

More and more tablet users are staying connected through text messages instead of phone calls, and the iPad Pro makes it easy to keep in touch with everyone. You can also use iMessage to interact with other Apple users. This feature allows you to send instant messages to anyone signed into a Mac running OS X Mountain Lion or higher, or any iOS device running iOS 5 or greater. iMessage for iPadOS has been completely changed to make everything just a little more…animated.

On the main Messages screen, you will be able to see the many different conversations you have going on. You can also delete conversations by swiping from right to left on the conversation you'd like and tapping the red Delete button. New conversations or existing conversations with new messages will be highlighted with a big blue dot next to it, and the Messages icon will have a badge displaying the number of unread messages you have, similar to the Mail and iPhone icons.

To create a message, click on the Messages icon, then the Compose button in the top right corner.

Once the new message dialog box pops up, click on the plus button (+) to choose from your contacts list, or just type in the phone number of the person you wish to text. For group messages, just keep adding as many people as you'd like. Finally, click on the bottom field to begin typing your message.

iMessage has added in a lot of new features over the past few years. If all you want to do is send a message, then just tap the blue up arrow.

But you can do so much more than just send a message! (Please note, if you are sending a message with newer features to someone with an older OS or a non-Apple device, then it won't look as it appears on your screen).

On the top of this screen, you'll also notice two tabs; one says "Bubble" and the other says "Screen"; if you tap Screen you can add animations to the entire screen. Swipe right and left to see each new animation.

When you get a message that you like, and you want to respond to it, you can tap and hold your finger over the message or image; this will bring up different ways you can react.

Once you make your choice, the person on the receiving end will see how you responded.

If you'd like to add animation, a photo, a video, or lots of other things, then let's look at the options next to the message.

You have three choices—which bring up even more choices! The first is the camera, which lets you send photos with your message (or take new photos—note, these photos won't be saved on your iPad Pro), the next lets you use iMessage apps (more on that in a second), and the last lets you record a message with your voice.

Let's look at the camera option first.

If you want to take an original photo, then tap the round button on the bottom. To add effects, tap the star in the lower left corner.

Tapping effects brings up all the different effects available to you. I'll talk more about Animoji soon but as an example, this app lets you put an Animoji over your face (see the example below— not bad for an author photo, eh?!)

Finally, the last option is apps. You should know all about iPad Pro apps by now, but now there's a new set of apps called iMessage apps. These apps let you be both silly (send digital stickers) and serious (send cash to someone via text). To get started, tap the '+' button to open the iMessage App Store.

You can browse all the apps just like you would the regular App Store. Installing them is the same as well.

When you're ready to use the app, just tap apps, tap the app you want to load, and tap what you want to send. You can also drag stickers on top of messages. Just tap, hold and drag.

Also, in the app section is a button called #images.

If you tap on this button you can search for thousands of humorous memes and animated GIFs. Just tap it and search a term you want to find—such as "Money" or "Fight".

One final iMessage feature worth trying out is the personal handwritten note. Tap on a new message like you are going to start typing a new message; now rotate your tablet horizontally. This brings up an option to use your finger to create a handwritten note. Sign away, and then hit done when you're finished.

Message Tagging

If you have used messaging programs like Slack, then you are probably all too familiar with tagging someone in a conversation. Tagging gets the person's attention and starts a new thread within the conversation.

So if you are in a large text message exchange, then when you tag someone, everyone can read it, but everyone is not notified. So it's a little less unobtrusive.

To tag someone in a conversation, just put an @ in front of their name when you reply.

If you want to reply in-line to a message, then long-press the message. By in-line, I mean this: let's say there's a message several texts up—you can long-press to reply to it, so they know what message you are referring to.

Once you tap Reply, you just reply as you normally would.

This is going to alert the person and they'll see the message with a reply notification under the message.

If it's several texts above, they'll also see it like the below message.

Pinning Messages

If you text a lot, then it might get a little cumbersome replying. The way Messages works is the most recent conversations go to the top. This mostly works well, but you can also pin favorites to the top.

In the example below, my wife is pinned to the top of the conversations. Even though other people have written me more recently, she will always be up there (unless I remove her). That makes it easy to reply.

To add or remove someone from the top, tap the Edit button in the upper left corner, then select Edit Pins (or swipe right over their message).

If you want to remove them, tap the minus icon above their photo (in the upper left corner); if you want to add them, tap the yellow pin icon.

You can have several people pinned to the top. Personally, I find three is good, but you can add even more.

Notifications

When you have your tablet locked, you'll start seeing notifications at some point; this tells you things like "You have a new email," "Don't forget to set your alarm," etc.

So, when you see all your notifications on your lock screen, they'll be organized by what they are. To see all the notifications from any one category, just tap it.

Not a fan of grouping? No problem. You can turn it off for any app. Head to Settings, then Notifications, then tap the app you want to turn grouping off for. Under Notification Groupings, just turn off automatic.

Using AirDrop

AirDrop was introduced in iOS 7, though Apple fans have likely used the Mac OS version on MacBooks and iMacs. In Mac OSX Sierra and Yosemite, you'll finally be able to share between iPadOS and your Mac using AirDrop.

AirDrop is Apple's file sharing service, and it comes standard on iPadOS 14 devices. You can activate AirDrop from the Share icon anywhere in iPadOS 14. If other AirDrop users are nearby, you'll see anything they're sharing in AirDrop, and they can see anything you share.

MULTITASKING

Multitasking has been on the iPad Pro since its release, but because many people are upgrading to iPad Pro from iPads, it's going to be a new feature for most.

There are three kinds of such multitasking:

Slide Over: (available on iPad Air, iPad Pro, iPad Air 2, iPad mini 2, iPad mini 3, and iPad mini 4) If you're working in one app, you can swipe from the right side of the screen to view and work with a second app; swipe down to pick a different app. This option is mainly if you want to check something quickly, but don't want to have the app running next to it. Notice how it hovers on top of it? You can slide back over to dismiss it.

To use it, open the app you want to run, then drag the app you want in Slide View to the right side.

This snaps it into side by side view (see below); from here, drag down from the top and it presents it in a Slide View.

Once it's in Slide Over view, you can drag other apps into that view and then toggle between them by sliding across the bottom edge of the view.

You can also swipe up from the bottom in this view to see all Slide Over windows that are open.

If you want to put any of these into full screen view drag the Slide Over view to the top center of the open full screen app.

Split View: (iPad Pro, iPad Air 2 and iPad mini 4) To keep two apps open at the same time, tap the app divider and drag it; this locks it onto the screen. Drag the divider to resize the app pane. To close it, slide the divider all the way to the right of the screen; this same method also lets you switch the app. This feature is supported on all Apple apps, but for other apps, it's up to the developer to include it. So, if you don't see a divider you can adjust, it just means the developer has not included this feature.

Picture in Picture: (iPad Air, iPad Air 2, iPad mini 2, iPad mini 3, and iPad mini 4) As a video plays (or during a FaceTime video call), press the Home button and the video scales down to a corner of your display. You can also pinch it with three fingers to shrink it.

Once it's shrunk, you can move it around your screen to any of the four corners.

If you want to close the video, tap the 'x'; if you want to enlarge it, tap the far-left button; and if you want to play it within another app, just open any app.

[5]
A Little More Than Basic

This chapter will cover:
- Sending email
- Surfing the Web
- Using iTunes
- Apple Music
- Finding apps on the App Store
- Adding Calendar items
- Using Maps
- Find My Friends
- Find My Phone
- Notes

Mail

The iPad Pro lets you add multiple email addresses from virtually any email client you can think of. Yahoo, Gmail, AOL, Exchange, Hotmail, and many more can be added to your iPad Pro so that you will be able to check your email no matter where you are. To add an email address, click on the Settings app icon, then scroll to the middle where you'll see Mail, Contacts & Calendar. You will then see logos for the biggest email providers, but if you have another type of email just click on Other and continue.

If you don't know your email settings, you will need to visit the Mail Settings Lookup page on the Apple website. There you can type in your entire email address, and the website will show you what information to type and where in order to get your email account working on the tablet. The settings change with everyone, so what works for one provider may not work with another. Once you are finished adding as many email accounts as you may need, you will be able to click on the Mail app icon on your tablet's Home screen and view each inbox separately, or all at once.

SURFING THE INTERNET WITH SAFARI

You've already seen how the address bar works. To search for something, you use the same exact box. That's how you can search for anything on the Internet. Think of it like a Google, Bing, or Yahoo! search engine in the corner of your screen. In fact, that's exactly what it is. Because when you search, it will use one of those search engines to find results.

On the bottom of the screen you'll see five buttons; the first two are back and forward buttons that make the website go either backwards or forwards to the website you were previously on.

Next to the address bar, is a button that lets you share a website, add it to the Home screen, print it, bookmark it, copy it, or add it to your reading list.

That's great! But what does it all mean? Let's look at each button on the menu:
Social Buttons: Mail, Message, Twitter, and Facebook are 'Social Buttons'; pressing any of them will share the website you are looking at with

whichever button you pressed (Message, FYI, is text message).

Add to Home Screen: If you go to a website frequently, this can be very convenient. What this button does is add an icon for that webpage right to your Home screen. That way whenever you want to launch the website, you can do it directly from the Home screen.

Print: If you have an AirPrint compatible printer, you can print a photo, document or webpage directly from your tablet.

Copy: This copies the website address.

Bookmark: If you go to a website often but don't want to add it to your Home screen then you can bookmark it. I will show you this in more detail in just a moment.

Add to Reading List: If you have a bunch of news stories open, you can add them to a Reading List to read later (even if you are offline).

Let's go back to the Bookmark button and see how that works.

When you add a bookmark (remember you do this from the previous button, the middle one), it will ask you to name it. By default, it will put it in the general bookmarks tab, but you can also create new folders by clicking on Bookmarks.

Now you can access the website anytime you want without typing the address by tapping on the Bookmarks button.

The iCloud tab is something you'll want to pay attention to if you use another Apple device (like an iPhone, an iPod Touch or a Mac computer). Your Safari browsing is automatically synced; so, if you are browsing a page on your iPhone, you can pick up where you left off on your iPad Pro.

The last button looks like a box on top of a transparent box.

If you use a computer or an older iPad; then you probably know all about tabs. Apple decided to not use tabs on Safari. Tabs are there in another way though, that's what this button is; it lets you have several windows open at the same time. When you press it, a new window appears. There's an option to open a New Page. Additionally, you can toggle between the pages that you already have open. Hitting the red 'x' will also close a page that you have opened. Hit Done to go back to normal browsing.

When you put your tablet in landscape (i.e. you turn it sideways), the browser also turns, and you will now have the option to use full screen mode. Tap the double arrows to activate it.

Reading List is the middle icon that looks like a pair of glasses where you can view all of the web pages, blog posts, or articles that you've saved for offline reading. To save a piece of internet literature to your reading list, tap on the Share icon and then click on Add to Reading List. Saved pages can be deleted like a text message by swiping from right to left and tapping on the red Delete button.

The third tab on the Bookmarks page is where you can view your shared links and subscriptions. Subscriptions can be created from any web page that provides RSS feeds, and your tablet will automatically download the latest articles and posts. To subscribe to a site's RSS, visit the website, tap the Bookmarks icon, and select Add to Shared Links.

Back on the main Safari home page, the last button found on the bottom right corner is Tabs. Just like the Mac version you can have multiple tabs of web pages open at the same time, and switch between them with ease. To switch the tabs into private mode where your browsing history or cookies will not be saved or recorded, tap the Tabs button and select Private. You will be asked to either close all existing tabs or keep them. If you don't want to lose any tabs that might still be open, opt to keep them. Existing tabs, in addition to any new tabs you open, will now be shielded behind private browsing.

SET YOUR DEFAULT EMAIL / WEB BROWSER

For a number of years, you were able to use other Mail and Web browsers in iOS, but you could not set it as a default. This changed in iOS 14…kind of. You can now have alternative default browsers and email clients, but the app has to be updated.

It's the developers (not Apple's) responsibility to update the app to take advantage of this feature; so when you try and change it using the steps below, and you don't see your preferred app, it's probably because either they haven't updated the app yet or you haven't updated the app yet (go to the App Store and make sure there's not an update for the app).

To change your preferred app, go to the Settings app. Next, go to the app you want to make the default (I'm using the Chrome browser in the example below); next, tap Default Browser.

Finally, check off your preferred browser. It saves automatically.

ITUNES

The iTunes app found on your Home screen opens the biggest digital music store in the world. You will be able to purchase and download not just music, but also countless movies, TV shows, audiobooks, and more. On the iTunes home page, you can also find a What's Hot section, collections of music, and new releases.

At the top, you will see the option to view either featured media or browse through the top charts. On the upper left corner is the Genres button. Clicking Genres will bring up many different types of music to help refine your search.

> Feature Alert: When you search a lyric in iTunes, it now brings back results.

Apple Music

Apple Music is a relatively new service from Apple that gives you the ability to stream the entire iTunes store and receive curated playlists from music experts tailored to your preferences. It costs $9.99 a month, but you can take advantage of the three-month free trial to see if this service is for you before paying for it. It also offers discount subscription pricing for family plans and college students.

Buying Apps

So how do you buy, download and finally remove apps? I'll look at that in this section.

To purchase apps, and I don't actually mean paying for them because you can purchase a free app without paying for it, follow the following:

The first thing you see when you open the App Store are the featured apps. This is to say games, lots and lots of games! Games are the top selling category in the App Store, but don't worry, there is more there than just games. Later in this handbook, I will tell you some of the essential apps you should get, but for now, let's see how the App Store works so that you discover some of them yourself.

If you hear about a new app and want to check it out, use the Search option.

When you find an app you want to buy, simply tap the price button and type in your App Store password. Remember that just because an app is free to download doesn't mean you won't have to pay something to use it. Many apps use 'in-app purchases' which means that you have to buy something within the app. You will be notified before you purchase anything though.

Apps are constantly coming out with updates like new, better features. Updates are almost always free, unless noted, and are easy to install. Just click on the last tab: Updates. If you have an app that needs to be updated, you will see it here. You will also see what's new in the app. If you see one, tap Update to begin the update.

If you bought an app, but accidentally deleted it, or changed your mind about deleting it, don't worry! You can download the app again in the same place that you see the updates. Just tap on Purchased.

When you tap the Purchased button, you will see two options: one is to see all the apps you have purchased and one to just see the apps that you have purchased but are not on your iPad Pro. Tap the one that says Not on This iPad to re-download anything, at no cost. Just tap the Cloud button to the right of the screen. You can even download it again if you bought it on another iPad as long as it's under the same account.

Deleting apps is easy; on your Home screen, tap and hold the icon of the app you want to remove, then tap the 'x' on top of the app.

Calendar

Among the other pre-installed apps that came with your new iPad Pro, perhaps one of the most used apps you'll encounter is the Calendar. You can switch between viewing appointments, tasks, or everything laid out in a one day, one week, or one month view.

Combine your calendar with email accounts or iCloud to keep your appointments and tasks synced across all of your devices, and never miss another appointment.

Creating an Appointment

To create an appointment, click on the Calendar icon on your Home screen. Click on whichever day you would like to set the appointment for, and then tap the '+' button in the corner. Here you will be able to name and edit your event, as well as connect it to an email or iCloud account in order to allow for syncing.

When editing your event, pay special attention to the duration of your event. Select the start and end times, or choose "All Day" if it's an all-day event. You will also have a chance to set it as a recurring event by clicking on Repeat and selecting how often you want it to repeat. In the case of a bill or car payment, for example, you could either select Monthly (on this day) or every 30 days, which are two different things. After you select your repetition, you can also choose how long you'd like for that event to repeat itself: for just one month, a year, forever, and everything in between.

Maps

The Maps app is back and better than ever. After Apple parted ways with Google Maps several years ago, Apple decided to develop its own, made-for-iPad map and navigation system. The result is a beautiful travel guide that takes full advantage of the newest iPad Pro resolutions. Full screen mode allows every corner of the tablet to be filled with the app, and there's an automatic night mode. You'll be able to search for places, restaurants, gas stations, concert halls, and other venues near you at any time, and turn-by-turn navigation is available for walking, biking, cycling, driving, or commuting. Traffic is updated in real time, so if an accident occurs ahead of you or there is construction going on, Maps will offer a faster alternative and warn you of the potential traffic jam.

The turn-by-turn navigation is easy to understand without being distracting, and the 3D view makes potentially difficult scenarios (like highway exits that come up abruptly) much more pleasant. Another convenient feature is the ability to avoid highways and toll roads entirely.

To set up navigation, tap on the Maps icon. On the bottom of the screen is a search for place or address; for homes you need an address, but businesses just need a name. Click on it and enter your destination once prompted.

When you find your destination's address, click on Route, and choose between walking or driving directions. For businesses, you also have the option of reading reviews and calling the company directly.

[screenshot of Disneyland Resort info page in Apple Maps]

For hands-free navigation, just say "Hey Siri" and say "Navigate to" or "Take me to" followed by the address or name of the location that you'd like to go to.

If you'd like to avoid highways or tolls, simply tap the More Options button and select the option that you want.

Apple Maps also lets you see a 3D view of thousands of locations. To enable this option, tap the 'i' in the upper right corner. After this, select satellite view.

If 3D view is available, you'll notice a change immediately. You can use two fingers to make your map more or less flat. You can also select 2D to remove 3D altogether.

Maps has taken big strides to compete against Google; in 2019, it added in a street level view to major cities like New York and Los Angeles with more expected soon. When you tap and hold on a location, you might notice it as an available view (if you don't see it, then it's not in that city yet).

When you tap on the view, then it gets larger.

Finally, similar to the iPhone version of Maps, iPad lets you add locations into collections so you can organize all of your favorite spots.

Map Guides

Map Guides are only available in larger cities. When you search for a city in the Map app, you will see the guides right under the directions button. You can also share the guide or save it.

As you look at the guides, it will show you recommendations on the map, and you can save them for later.

Find My

If you used Find My Phone or Find My Friend on previous OSes, then shocker: they're gone! These two powerful apps let you see where your friends were on a map or where your devices were on a map.

They're essentially the same app with a different purpose; so instead of keeping both, Apple decided to delete them and combine them into one app called Find My.

![Find My]

The app is pretty simple. Three tabs on the bottom. One to find your friends (i.e. People), one to find your devices, and one to change settings (i.e. Me).

If you want to see where your friend is at, ask them to share their location with you in the People section.

It's not very helpful using an app to find your iPad if you don't have your iPad. If that's the case, you can also use your computer browser to see it at iCloud.com.

Notes

The Notes app has always been the go-to app for jotting down quick and simple notes—it's like Word or Pages, but without all the fancy stuff. In iPadOS, Notes is still simple—but it got a whole lot fancier...while retaining the simplicity that people love about it.

At first glance, Notes looks basically the same as it always has. Notice that little plus sign above the keyboard? That's what's different.

Tap the '+' button one time, and you'll see the options that have been added.

Starting from the left side is a checkmark, which is what you press if you'd like to make a checklist instead of a note. For each new checkmark, just tap the return button on the keyboard.

○ Check list
○ Item 2
○ Item 3

The 'Aa' button is what you would press if you would like to format the note a little (larger fonts, bold, bulleted text, etc.).

Formatting

Title

Heading

Body ✓

• Bulleted List

– Dashed List

The little camera button will let you add a photo you have taken or let you take a photo from within the app and insert it.

Photo Library

Take Photo or Video

Cancel

And finally, the squiggly line lets you draw in the Notes app; when you press it, you'll see three different brushes (pen, marker, and pencil) that each work a little differently, as well as a ruler and eraser.

There's also a round black circle—tapping that lets you change the color of the brush.

Just tap the Done button in the upper right corner once you've picked your color and it will be changed.

Once you tap the Done button after you've finished drawing, you will go back to the note. If you tap the drawing, however, it will activate it again and you can make changes or add to your drawing.

○ Check list
○ Item 2
○ Item 3

Hello

It's obviously not the most advance drawing app—but that's the point—it's not supposed to be. As the name of the app says, this app is just for jotting or drawing quick notes.

In the Settings menu a Search option has been added at the top. There are a lot of Settings in iOS and there are more and more with each update—Search Settings let you quickly access the setting you want. So, for instance, if you want to stop getting notifications for a certain app, you no longer have to thumb through endless apps—now just search for it.

Settings

Q Search Settings

Airplane Mode

Notes has also been added to Safari, so if you want to add a website to a note, it's now possible.

Whenever you see the option to use Markup you will be using Notes interface.

SEARCH TEXT IN APP

When you swipe down from the middle of the screen, you can quickly search for apps, which is helpful if you have a lot of them. You can also search for text within apps by scrolling down to the section titled "Search in Apps."

[6]
CUSTOMIZING

This chapter will cover:
- Screen Time
- Do Not Disturb Mode
- Notifications and Widgets
- General Settings
- Sounds
- Customizing Brightness and Wallpaper
- Adding Facebook, Twitter and Flickr Accounts
- Family Sharing
- Continuity and Handoff

Now that you know your way around, it's time to dig into the settings and make this tablet completely custom to you!

For most of this chapter, I'll be hanging out in the Settings area, so if you aren't already there, tap Settings from your Home screen.

Screen Time

To use Screen Time, head on into Settings > Screen Time

You can click on any app to see how much time you've spent in it, and even what your average is. From here you can also add limits.

Do Not Disturb Mode

Do Not Disturb mode is a handy feature located near the top of your Settings app. When this operational mode is enabled, you won't receive any notifications and all of your calls will be silenced. This is a useful trick for those times when you can't afford to be distracted (and let's face it, your iPad Pro is as communicative as they come, and sometimes you'll need to have some peace and quiet!). Clock alarms will still sound.

To turn on, schedule and customize Do Not Disturb, just tap on Do Not Disturb in Settings. You can schedule automatic times to activate this feature, like your work hours, for example. You can also specify certain callers who should be allowed when your tablet is set to Do Not Disturb. This way, your mother can still get through, but you won't have to hear every incoming email. To do this, use the Allow Call From command in Do Not Disturb settings.

Do Not Disturb is also accessible through the Control Center (swipe down from the upper right corner of the screen to access it at any time).

NOTIFICATIONS AND WIDGETS

Notifications are one of the most useful features on the iPad Pro, but chances are you won't need to be informed of every single event that's set as a default in your Notifications Center. To adjust Notifications preferences, go to Settings > Notifications.

By tapping the app, you can turn Notifications off or on and finesse the type of notification from each app. It's a good idea to whittle this list down to the apps that you truly want to be notified from—for example, if you're not an investor, turn off Stocks! Reducing the number of sounds your iPad Pro makes can also reduce tablet-related frazzledness. For example, in Mail, you may want your tablet to make a sound when you receive email from someone on your VIP list but to only display badges for other, less important email.

General Settings

The General menu item is a little bit of a catchall. This is where you'll find information about your iPad Pro, including its current version of iOS and any available software updates. Fortunately, iPadOS 14 ushers in an era of smaller, more efficient updates, so you won't find yourself scrambling to delete apps in order to make space for the latest improvements. You can also check your tablet and iCloud storage here.

The Accessibility options are located here as well. You can set your iPad Pro according to your needs with Zoom, Voiceover, large text, color adjustment, and more. There are a quite a few Accessibility options that can make iPadOS 14 easy for everyone to use, including Grayscale View and improved Zoom options.

A handy Accessibility option that's a little disguised is the AssistiveTouch setting. This gives you a menu that helps you access device-level functions. Enabling it brings up a floating menu designed to help users who have difficulty with screen gestures like swiping or with manipulating the iPad Pro's physical buttons. Another feature for those with visual needs is Magnifier. Turning this on allows your camera to magnify things, and you can also click the Home button on older models and magnify anything that you're looking at.

I recommend taking some time and tapping through the General area, just so you know where everything is!

SOUNDS

Hate that vibration when your tablet rings? Want to change your ring tone? Head to the Sounds Settings menu! Here you can turn vibration on or off and assign ring tones to a number of iPad Pro functions. I do suggest finding an isolated space before you start trying out all the different sound settings—it's fun, but possibly a major annoyance to those unlucky enough not to be playing with their own new iPad Pro!

Tip: You can apply individual ringtones and message alerts to your contacts. Just go to the person's contact screen in Contacts, tap Edit, and tap Assign Ringtone.

CUSTOMIZING BRIGHTNESS AND WALLPAPER

On the iPad Pro, wallpaper refers to the background image on your Home screen and to the image displayed when your iPad Pro is locked (Lock screen). You can change either image using two methods.

For the first method, visit Settings > Wallpapers. You'll see a preview of your current wallpaper and Lock screen here. Tap Choose a New Wallpaper. From there, you can choose a pre-loaded dynamic (moving) or still image, or choose one of your own photos. Once you've chosen an image, you'll see a preview of the image as a Lock screen. Here, you can turn off Perspective Zoom (which makes the image appear to shift as you tilt your tablet) if you like. Tap Set to continue. Then choose whether to set the image as the Lock screen, Home screen, or both.

The other way to make the change is through your Photo app. Find the photo you'd like to set as a wallpaper image and tap the Share button. You'll be given a choice to set an image as a background, a Lock screen, or both.

If you want to use images from the web, it's fairly easy. Just press and hold the image until the Save Image / Copy / Cancel message comes up. Saving the image will save it to your Recently Added photos in the Photos app.

Privacy

The Privacy heading in Settings lets you know what apps are doing with your data. Every app you've allowed to use Location Services will show up under Location Services (and you can toggle Location Services off and on for individual apps or for your whole device here as well). You can also go through your apps to check what information each one is receiving and transmitting.

When you are using any app that is using either the camera or microphone, you will now see a green indicator just above your cellular signal bar.

Compromised Password

Data breaches are pretty common these days; Apple is doing its part to be transparent about when they happen and help you fix it before it's a problem.

Go to the Settings app, then scroll until you get to Passwords.

Within this area (which is password protected) you can see all your stored passwords, but under Security Recommendations, you can also see if your password "may" have been compromised. I say "may" because this does not mean you have been hacked. It just means some data from a company was taken, and you might be on that list because you've had an account there in the past.

When you click the recommendations, it will take you one by one to each possible breach and show you why it's making the recommendation. In the example below, it says Apple had a breach and they are suggesting I change my password.

I can tap the Change Password on Website to change the password, or I can click the message to read a little more about it. In the example below, it's saying that it noticed I used the same password on another website, so I should change that one as well.

Privacy Report

In Safari, you can tap the AA icon next to the web address to see a Privacy Report.

The Privacy Report will tell me more about trackers that have been trying to follow me. A tracker is basically a little code embedded in a website to follow what I do. For example, it tells Facebook that I've visited a website about Legos, so it should start showing me Lego ads. Creepy, right?!

Mail, Contacts, Calendars Settings

If you need to add additional Mail, Contacts or Calendar accounts, tap Settings > Mail, Contacts and Calendars to do so. It's more or less the same process as adding a new account in-app. You can also adjust other settings here, including your email signature for each linked account. This is also a good place to check which aspects of each account are linked—for example, you may want to link your Tasks, Calendars and Mail from Exchange, but not your Contacts. You can manage all of this here.

There are a number of other useful settings here, including the frequency you want your accounts to check for mail (Push, the default, being the hardest on your battery life). You can also turn on features like Ask Before Deleting and adjust the day of the week you'd like your calendar to start on.

ADDING FACEBOOK AND TWITTER

If you use Twitter, Facebook or Flickr, you'll probably want to integrate them with your iPad Pro. This is a snap to do. Just tap on Settings and look for Twitter, Facebook and Flickr in the main menu (you can also integrate Vimeo and Weibo accounts if you have them). Tap on the platform you want to integrate. From there, you'll enter your username and password. Doing this will allow you to share webpages, photos, notes, App Store pages, music and more, straight from your iPad Pro's native apps.

iPad Pro will ask you if you'd like to download the free Facebook, Twitter and Flickr apps when you configure your accounts if you haven't already done so. I recommend doing this—the apps are easy to use, free, and look great.

I have found that when I associated my Facebook account, my contacts list got extremely bloated. If you don't want to include your Facebook friends in your contacts list, adjust the list of applications that can access your Contacts in Settings > Facebook.

FAMILY SHARING

Family Sharing is one of my favorite iPadOS 14 features. Family Sharing allows you to share App Store and iTunes purchases with family members (previously, accomplishing this required a tricky and not-entirely-in-compliance-with-terms-of-service dance). Turning on Family Sharing also creates a shared family calendar, photo album, and reminder list. Family members can also see each other's location in Apple's free Find My app and check the location of each other's devices. Overall, Family Sharing is a great way to keep everyone entertained and in sync! You can include up to six people in Family Sharing.

To enable Family Sharing, go to Settings > iCloud. Here, tap Set Up Family Sharing to get started. The person who initiates Family Sharing for a family is known as the family organizer. It's an important role, since every purchase made by family members will be made using the family organizer's credit card! Once you set up your family, they'll also be able to download your past purchases, including music, movies, books, and apps.

Invite your family members to join Family Sharing by entering their Apple IDs. As a parent, you can create Apple IDs for your children with parental consent. When you create a new child Apple ID, it is automatically added to Family Sharing.

There are two types of accounts in Family Sharing—adult and child. As you'd expect, child accounts have more potential restrictions than adult accounts do. Of special interest is the Ask to Buy option. This prevents younger family members from running up the family organizer's credit card bill by requiring parental authorization for purchases. The family organizer can also designate other adults in the family as capable of authorizing purchases on children's devices.

Creating Custom Shortcuts

If you want to put your own fresh spin on any icon, it's "technically" possible, but there are limitations. For example, you could change the iMessage icon to your wedding photo. What are the limitations? You will not get notification indicators on it. So your icon won't light up with a new message indicator, for example. It also launches through the Shortcuts app, which creates a delay for how quickly it opens.

To do this, you need to create a Shortcut for the app. If you don't see the Shortcuts app, then it's possible that you deleted it and need to install it again.

When the app launches, tap the + icon in the upper right corner.

Next, select Add Action.

You can search for all possible actions, but it's faster just to search for the actions you want to perform. In this case: Open app.

Tap Choose to select the app you want to open.

```
SCRIPTING
Open  Choose

Cancel          Choose App
Q Search Apps
    A Design Kit
    APL LIBRARY
    App Store
    Baby Monitor
    Books
    Camera
```

Type in the name of the app you want to open. I'm choosing the Messages app.

Next, tap the icon in the upper right corner with the three dots and blue circle.

You want to create an icon for it on your Home screen, so tap Add to Home Screen.

Tap the icon image, and select where the image is that you want to use, then select the image.

It will give you a preview of the icon. Before tapping Done, make sure and change the name from New Shortcut to whatever you want to call it.

Once you finish, it will show up on your Home screen just like any other app.

Continuity and Handoff

iPadOS 14 includes some incredible features for those of us who work on multiple iPadOS 14 and Sierra and Yosemite OSX devices. Now, when your computer is running Yosemite or higher or your iPadOS 14 iPad is connected to the same Wi-Fi network as your iOS 13 iPhone, you can answer calls or send text messages (both iMessages and regular SMS messages) from your iPad or computer.

The Handoff feature is present in apps like Numbers, Safari, Mail and many more. Handoff allows you to leave an app on one device mid-action and pick up right where you left off on a different device. It makes life much easier for those of us living a multi-gadget lifestyle.

[7]
THE CAMERA

This chapter will cover:
- Taking photos and videos
- Editing photos
- Sharing photos and videos

TAKING PHOTOS AND VIDEOS

Now that you know how to make a tablet call, let's get back to the fun stuff! I'll look at using the Photo app next.

The Camera app is on your Home screen, but you can also get to it from your Lock screen for quick, easy access.

The Camera app is pretty simple to use. First, you should know that the Camera app has two cameras; one on the front and one on the back.

The front camera has a lower resolution and is mostly used for self-portraits; it still takes excellent photos, but just remember the back camera is better. To access it, tap the button in the top right corner (the one with the camera and two arrows). The bar on the bottom has all your camera modes. This is how you can switch from photo to video mode.

On the side of the screen you will see a lightning button. That's your flash. Tap this button and you can toggle between different flash modes.

The next two buttons you won't use quite as much. The first, the circle, is for live photos. Live photos takes a short video while you take the photo; it's so quick you won't even know it did it. It's on automatically, so tap it once to turn it off; if you tap and hold a photo with live photo enabled, then you will see the video. Next to that is a timer, which, as you might expect, delays the shot so you can take a group photo.

One of the photo modes is called "Pano" or Panorama. Panorama is the ability to take an extra-long photo that's over 20 megapixels in size. To use it tap the Panorama button. On-screen instructions will now appear. Simply press the Shoot button at the bottom of the screen, and rotate the camera as straight as possible while following the line. When it reaches the end, the photo will automatically go into your album.

The mode you've probably seen the most about is Portrait mode. Portrait mode gives your photos that blurred effect you see on high-end DSLR cameras.

Whether a user is a selfie lover or a photo portrait addict, these are two features all users will appreciate.

To access and use Portrait mode and Portrait Light mode on the iPad Pro:

Bring up the Camera app.

Swipe up or down to switch to the Portrait setting.

Line up the shot within 2-8 feet of the subject. The camera's face and body detection will automatically identify the subject and provide instruction to move further or get closer to the subject.

Pay attention to the Camera app's prompts: more light required, flash may help, place subject within 8 feet, or move farther away.

When the shot is ready a banner will appear at the bottom.

Swipe or tap on the cube icons above the shutter button to change lighting effects.

Press the Shutter button to take the photo.

Note: Users can still shoot with the telephoto lens in Portrait mode even if the banners don't turn yellow—it just means a lesser depth or lighting effect.

There are several different Portrait modes (Studio Lighting, for example), but you can switch modes after you take the photo; so, if you take it with Studio Lighting, but decide another mode would look better, then you can change it.

> **Feature Alert**: The newest iPad Pros can now adjust the depth of the blur after the photo is taken. To do this, just select Edit after the shot is taken. This only works for photos taken with Portrait mode.

Photo Editing

Editing your photos is just as easy as taking them. As simple as editing tools are, they are also quite powerful. If you want more power though, you can always download one of the hundreds of photo editing apps in the App Store.

To edit a photo, tap the Photo icon on your Home screen.

When you launch Photos, you will see a tab with three buttons; right now, I'll be talking about the Photos button, but we'll talk about Photo Stream in the next chapter. Tap Albums and let's get editing!

Next, tap the photo you want to edit and then tap Edit in the upper-right corner. This will open the editing menu. On the bottom of the screen, you will see all the options: undo, auto correct (which corrects the color of the photo), color change, red eye removal, and finally crop.

The only added feature is the middle one, which lets you change the color saturation.

When you are satisfied with the changes tap Save in the upper right corner.

Remember, whenever you want to get to the previous screen just tap the Back button in the upper-left corner.

Live Photos

Apple introduced Live Photos in 2015, when the iPhone 6s came out. This feature enhances the tablets photography, using pictures that move. iPadOS 14 makes Live Photos better than ever. Wanna know how to take a live photo? Let's have a look.

Live Photos records what happens 1.5 seconds before and after you take the photo. That means you're not only getting a photo, you're also getting movement and sound.

Open the Camera app;

Set your camera to Photo mode, and turn Live Photos on;

Hold the tablet very still;

Tap ⭕.

With your iPad Pro, Live Photos is naturally on by default. If you want to take a still image, tap ⭕ and you'll be allowed to turn off Live Photos. If you want Live Photos to always be off, go to Settings > Camera > Preserve Settings.

Photo Albums and Photo Sharing

So now that your photo is taken and edited, let's see how to share photos.

There are several ways to share photos. When you open a photo, you will see an option bar on the bottom. The older version had more options—these options have now been moved to one central place, which you will see next.

The first button lets you share the photo socially and to media devices.

The top row is more of the social options; the bottom row is more of the media options. AirPlay, for example, let's you wirelessly send the photos if you have an Apple TV.

Finally, the last button lets you delete the photo, don't worry about accidently deleting a photo, because it asks you to confirm if you want to delete the photo before you delete it.

Next, let's go to the middle tab. Photo Stream is sort of like Flickr; it lets you share your photos with your family and friends easily. To get to Photo Stream, tap the Shared button on the bottom of the Photo app.

On the top left corner is a '+' button; tap it.

This brings up a menu that lets you create a shared directory. From there you can choose the name, who sees it and if it's a public or private photo stream. To choose a person in your contacts tap the blue '+' button.

Once the album is created, tap the '+' button and tap on each photo you want to add, then hit done.

Once your family or friend accepts your Stream invitation, you will automatically begin syncing your photos. Anytime you add a photo to your album, they will receive a notification.

The new iPadOS will now also group your photos as memories; it does this by looking at where the photo was taken and when it was taken. So, you'll start noticing groups like "Christmas Memories."

Photo Captioning

Swiping up on a photo lets you make changes and add filters, and it also lets you add a caption; captions can later be searched. So you can add something like "Grand Canyon Vacation" and later search for that term.

Hide Photos

We all have embarrassing photos—you know, the ones with you dressed in a tutu while riding a unicorn? Or is that just me?!

If you want to hide "certain" photos so only you can see them, then that's an option. It used to be you could hide them, but they would show up in your albums. They were "kind of" hidden, but I think most people would agree that they weren't so much hidden as harder to find.

In iPadOS 14, the ability was added to completely hide that folder. Go to the Settings app, and then Photos; scroll to Hidden Album. If it's toggled on, the Hidden Album will be in the Utilities area of albums (like I said, harder to find, but not really hidden); if it's toggled off, it's gone. Like nowhere to be found. The images are saved and stored in the cloud—even though you can't see them. To see them, toggle it back on, then go to Albums and scroll to Utilities. If you know a celebrity, then pass this information on to them, so we can stop hearing about all those "accidental" shares of photos meant to be private.

To hide a photo, find it, then select it and tap the Share icon; this brings up how you want to share it (kind of a misleading name, isn't it—you're hiding it because you don't want to share it!); one of the options is Hide—tap that.

It will confirm that you actually want to hide it. If you change your mind later, then you go into the hidden album and unhide it the same way. You can also select several images at a time to hide them as a group.

[8]
Animoji?

> This chapter will cover:
> - What is Animoji?
> - How to use Animoji

How to Add Your Own Animoji

I'm going to be honest, I think Animoj is creepy! What is it? You almost have to try it to understand it. In a nutshell, Animoji turns you into an emoji. Want to send someone an emoji of a monkey? That's fun. But you know else is fun? Making that monkey have the same expression as you!

When you use Animoji, you put the camera in front of you. If you put out your tongue, the emoji sticks out it's tongue. If you wink, the emoji winks. So, it's a way to send a person an emoji with exactly how you are feeling.

To use it, open your iMessage app. Start a text the way you normally would. Tap the App button followed by the Animoji button. Choose an Animoji and tap to see full screen. Look directly into the camera and place your face into the fame. Tap the record button and speak for up to 10 seconds. Tap the Preview button to look at the Animoji. Tap the Upward Arrow button to send or the Trashcan to delete.

You can also create an emoji that looks like you. Click that big '+' button next to the other Animojis.

This will walk you through all the steps to send your very own custom Animoji—from hair color to type of nose.

When you're done, you are ready to send.

[9]
Hey, Siri

> This chapter will cover:
> - Siri

By now, you probably know all about Siri and how it can remind you of things. If not, say, "Hey, Siri."

Siri works the same as always, but she's gotten a few under-the-hood updates to make her faster.

The biggest change to Siri is the look. The theme of many of the changes to iOS is how do you minimize what already works. With Siri that means having a smaller look. It now launches in a more nonintrusive way.

Her replies also go with fewer distractions. She used to launch full-screen replies that took you out of what you were doing to see the answer. Now it just takes a little bit of space.

So, what exactly do you do with it? The first thing you should do is introduce Siri to your family. Siri is pretty smart, and she wants to meet your family. To introduce her to your family, activate Siri and say: "Brian is my brother" or "Susan is my boss." Once you confirm the relationship you can now say things like: "Call my brother" or "email my boss."

Siri is also location-based. What does that mean? It means that instead of saying: "Remind me to call wife at 8 am" you can say: "Remind me when I leave work to call wife" and as soon as you step out of the office you will receive a reminder. Siri can be a bit frustrating at first, but it's one of the tablet's most powerful apps, so give it a chance!

Everyone hates dealing with waits. There's nothing worse than being hungry and having to wait an hour for a table. Siri does her best to make your life easier by making reservations for you. For this to work, you'll need a free app called OpenTable (you'll also need a free account), which is in the Apple App Store. This app makes its money by restaurants paying it, so don't worry about having to pay to use it. Once it's installed, you will simply activate Siri and say: "Hey Siri, make me a reservation at the Olive Garden," (or wherever you want to eat). Note that not all restaurants participate in OpenTable, but hundreds (if not thousands) do, and it's growing monthly, so if it's not there it probably will be soon.

Siri is ever evolving. And with the latest update, Apple has taught her everything she needs to know about sports. Go ahead, try it! Say something like: "Hey, Siri. What's the score in the Kings game?" or: "Who leads the league in homeruns?"

Siri has also got a little wiser in movies. You can say: "Movies directed by Peter Jackson" and it will give you a list and let you see a synopsis, the review rating from Rotten Tomatoes, and in some cases even a trailer or an option to buy the movie. You can also say: "Movie show times" and a list of nearby movies playing will appear. At this time, you cannot buy tickets to the movie, though one can imagine that option will be coming very soon.

Finally, Siri can open apps for you. If you want to open an app, simply say: "Open and the apps name."

The new iPadOS lets you add shortcuts to Siri; you can see this in Settings > Siri & Search > Shortcuts.

[10]
APPLE SERVICES

This chapter will cover:
- iCloud
- Apple Arcade
- Apple TV+
- Apple Music
- Apple News
- Apple Card

INTRODUCTION

It used to be a few times a year Apple would take the stage and announce something that everyone's head exploded over! The iPhone! The iPad! The Apple Watch! The iPod!

That still happens today, but Apple also is well aware of the reality: most people don't upgrade to new hardware every year. How does a company make money when that happens? In a word: services.

In the past few years (especially in 2019) Apple announced several services—things people would opt into to pay for monthly. It was a way to continue making money even when people were not buying hardware.

For it to work, Apple knew they couldn't just offer a subpar service and expect people to pay because it said Apple. It had to be good. And it is!

This book will walk you through those services and show you how to get the most out of them.

ICLOUD

iCloud is something that Apple doesn't talk a lot about but is perhaps their biggest service. It's estimated that nearly 850 million people use it. The thing about it, however, is many people don't even know they're using it.

What exactly is it? If you are familiar with Google Drive, then the concept is something you probably already understand. It's an online storage locker. But it's more than that. It is a place where you can store files, and it also syncs everything—so if you send a message on your iPhone, it appears on your MacBook and iPad. If you work on a Keynote presentation from your iPad, you can continue where you left off on your iPhone.

What's even better about iCloud is it's affordable. New phones get 5GB for free. From there the price range is as follows (note that these prices may change after printing):
- 50GB: $0.99
- 200GB: $2.99
- 2TB: $9.99

These prices are for everyone in your family. So, if you have five people on your plan, then each person doesn't need their own storage plan. This also means purchases are saved—if one family member buys a book or movie, everyone can access it.

iCloud has become even more powerful as our photo library grows. Photos used to be relatively small, but as cameras have advanced, the size goes up. Most photos on your phone are several MB big. iCloud means you can keep the newest ones on your phone and put the older ones in the Cloud. It also means you don't have to worry about paying for the phone with the biggest hard drive—in fact, even if you have the biggest hard drive, there's a chance it won't fit all of your photos.

Where Is iCloud?
If you look at your iPad, you won't see an iCloud app. That's because there isn't an iCloud app. There's a Files app that functions like a storage locker.

To see iCloud, point your computer browser to iCloud.com.

Once you sign in, you'll see all the things stored in your Cloud—photos, contacts, notes, files; these are all things you can access across all of your devices.

In addition, you can use iCloud from any computer (even PCs); this is especially helpful if you need to use Find My, which locates not only your iPhone, but all of your Apple devices—phones, watches, even AirPods.

Backing Up Your Phone With iCloud
The first thing you should know about iCloud is how to back up your phone with it. This is what you will need to do if you are moving from one phone to another.

If there's no iCloud app on the phone, then how do you do that? While there is no native app in the traditional sense that you are used to, there are several iCloud settings in the Settings app.

Open the Settings app; at the top you will see your name and profile picture; tap that.

Settings

Scott
Apple ID, iCloud, iTunes & App Store

This opens my ID settings where I can update things like phone numbers and email. One of the options is iCloud. Tap that.

Name, Phone Numbers, Email
Password & Security
Payment & Shipping
Subscriptions

iCloud
iTunes & App Store
Find My
Family Sharing

Scroll down a little until you get to the setting that says iCloud Backup, and tap that.

> Wallet
> Game Center
> Siri
> Keychain   On >
> iCloud Backup   On >
> iCloud Drive

It will probably be on (the toggle switch will be green); if you'd rather do things manually, then you can toggle it off and then do Back Up Now. If you turn it off, then you'll have to do a manual backup each time.

> BACKUP
> iCloud Backup
> Automatically back up data such as your accounts, documents, Home configuration, and settings when this iPhone is connected to power, locked, and on Wi-Fi. Learn more...
>
> Back Up Now
> You must be connected to a Wi-Fi network to start a backup.
> Last successful backup: 3:00 AM

From the iCloud, you'll also be able to change what apps use iCloud and see how much space you have left. In my case, I have the 2TB plan, and we've used about half of it.

> **STORAGE**
> iCloud — 773.5 GB of 2 TB Used
> ● Photos ● Docs ● Others ● Family
> Manage Storage >
>
> **APPS USING ICLOUD**
> Photos — On >

If you tap Manage Storage, you can see where the storage is being used. You can also upgrade or downgrade your account from this page by tapping on Change Storage Plan.

> iCloud — 773.5 GB of 2 TB Used
> ● Photos ● Docs ● Others ● Family
>
> Family Usage — 377.3 GB >
> Change Storage Plan — 2 TB >
>
> Photos — 184.4 GB >

Tap on Family Usage and you can see more specifically which family members use what. You can also stop sharing from this page.

Moving to a New Device

When you get a new device, you will be asked during the setup to log in with your Apple ID associated with your previous device, and then get the option to recover from a previous device.

Sharing Photos With iCloud

To share and backup photos with iCloud, go into Settings > Photos and ensure iCloud Photos is toggled to green. If you are short on storage, you can check the option below to Optimize Storage.

Files App

To see your cloud files, open the Files app.

The first thing you'll see is all your recent files.

If you don't see what you are looking for, then go to the bottom tabs and switch from Recents to Browse.

This opens a more traditional looking file explorer.

If you want to create a new folder, connect to a server, or scan a document, tap and hold anywhere on your screen.

Scan Documents lets you use your camera like a traditional flatbed scanner to scan and print documents.

You can also access this option by tapping on locations, then tapping on the three small dots.

You can drag up from the top to reveal a hidden sort menu (where you can also create a new folder).

Tapping and holding on any of the icons will reveal a menu option that lets you share, rename, and more to a file.

| Copy |
| Duplicate |
| Move |
| Delete |
| Info |
| Quick Look |
| Tags |
| Rename |
| Share |
| Compress |
| Download |

iCloud Settings

One other important set of iCloud settings is in Settings > General > iPad Storage.

When you tap this, it will show you how much storage apps are using and also make recommendations.

Apple Music

Apple Music is Apple's music streaming service. The question most people wonder is which is better: Spotify or Apple Music? On paper it's hard to tell. They both have the same number of songs, and they both cost the same ($9.99 a month, $5 for students, $14.99 for families).

There really is no clear winner. It all comes down to preference. Spotify has some good features—such as an ad-supported free plan.

One of the standout features of Apple Music is iTunes Match. If you are like me and have a large collection of audio files on your computer, then you'll love iTunes Match. Apple puts those files in the Cloud, and you can stream them on any of your devices. This feature is also available if you don't have Apple Music for $25 a year.

Apple Music also plays well with Apple devices; so, if you are an Apple house (i.e. everything you own, from smart speakers to TV media boxes, has the Apple logo), then Apple Music is probably the best one for you.

Apple is compatible with other smart speakers, but it's built to shine on its own devices.

I won't cover Spotify here, but my advice is to try them both (they both have free trials) and see which interface you prefer.

Apple Music Crash Course

Before going over where things are in Apple Music, it's worth noting that Apple Music can now be accessed from your web browser (in beta form) here: http://beta.music.apple.com.

It's also worth noting that I have a little girl and don't get to listen to a lot of "adult" music, so the examples here are going to show a lot of kids music!

The main navigation on Apple Music is at the bottom. There are five basic menus to select from:
- Library
- For You

- Browse
- Radio
- Search

At the far right is a bar with what's currently playing (if applicable).

Library
When you create playlists or download songs or albums, this is where you will go to find them.

You can change the categories that show up in this first list by tapping on Edit, then checking off the categories you want. Make sure to hit Done to save your changes.

For You

As you play music, Apple Music starts to get to know you more and more; it makes recommendations based on what you are playing.

In For You, you can get a mix of all these songs and see other recommendations.

In addition to different styles of music, it also has friends' recommendations so you can discover new music based on what your friends are listening to.

Browse

Not digging those recommendations? You can also browse genres in the Browse menu. In addition to different genre categories, you can see what music is new and what music is popular.

Radio

Radio is Apple's version of AM/FM; the main radio station is Beats One. There are on-air DJs and everything you'd expect from a radio station.

While Beats One is Apple's flagship station, it's not its only station. You can scroll down and tap on Radio Stations under More to explore and see several other stations based on music styles (i.e. country, alternative, rock, etc.). Under this menu, you'll also find a handful of talk stations covering news and sports. Don't expect to find the opinionated talk radio you may listen to on regular radio—it's pretty controversy-free.

Search
The last option is the search menu, which is pretty self-explanatory. Type in what you want to find (i.e. artist, album, genre, etc.).

Listening to Music and Creating a Playlist
You can access the music you are currently listening to from the bottom of your screen.

Tapping on this brings up a larger view of what you are listening to with several options.

The play, back/forward, and volume buttons are pretty straightforward. The buttons below that might look new.

The first option is for lyrics. If the song is paused, then you can read through the lyrics; if the song is playing, then it will bold the lyrics to the song it is currently playing. If you ever caught yourself wondering if the singer is saying "dense" or "dance" then this feature is a game changer.

The middle option lets you pick where you play the music. For example, if you have a HomePod and you want to listen wirelessly to the music from that device, you can change it here.

The last option shows the next song(s) in the playlist.

If you want to add a song to a playlist, then click the three dots next to the album/artist name. This brings up a list of several options (you can also go here to love or hate a song—which helps Apple Music figure out what you like); the option you want is Add to a Playlist. If you don't have a playlist or want to add it to a new one, then you can also create one here.

At any point, you can tap the artist's name to see all of their music.

In addition to seeing information about the band, their popular songs, and their albums, you can get a playlist of their essential songs or a playlist of bands that they have influenced.

If you scroll to the bottom, you can also see Similar Artists, which is a great way to discover new bands that are like the ones you are currently listening to.

Tips for Getting the Most Out of Apple Music

HEART IT

Like what you're hearing? Heart it! Hate it? Dislike it. Apple gets to know you by what you listen to, but it improves the accuracy when you tell it what you think of a song you are really into...or really hate.

USE SETTINGS

Some of the most resourceful features of Apple Music aren't in Apple Music—they're in your settings.

Open the Settings app and scroll down to Music.

Want to change the way your music sounds—such as more or less bass—go to EQ in the settings.

DOWNLOAD MUSIC

If you don't want to rely on data when you are on the go, make sure and tap the cloud on your music to download the music locally to your phone. If you don't see a cloud, add it to your library by tapping the plus, which should change it to a cloud.

HEY SIRI

Siri knows music! Say "Hey Siri," and say what you want to listen to, and the AI will get to work.

APPLE NEWS

In 2012, a little app with big ambitions called Next (it was later changed to Texture) disrupted the magazine industry by creating the Netflix of magazines. For one low price, you could read hundreds of magazines (and their back issues, too). They weren't small indie magazines—they were the big ones: People, Time, Wired, and more.

Apple took notice, and, in 2018, they acquired the company. The writing was on the wall: Apple wanted to get into print services.

In 2019, it was announced that Texture would close because Apple would release a new service called News+. News+ does everything that Texture did, but also combines newspapers (Los Angeles Times and The Wall Street Journal).

There is a free version of the service that curates news for you; the paid version that carries the magazine subscriptions is $9.99. (You can have five family members on your plan.)

What really makes Apple News stand out is it's curated for you and your tastes. If you have other family members on your plan, it will be curated for them as well—it's based on the user's tastes, so if you have a family member into entertainment news and you are into game news, you won't see their interests—only yours.

Apple News Crash Course

To get started, open the News app from your iPad (if it is not on your iPad, it's a free download from the App Store).

The UI for the app is pretty simple. There are several menu options found by swiping from the left of the screen to the right; the two you will use the most:

Today—This is where you'll find your curated news

News+—Where you'll find magazines

Today

The Today menu gives you all your news (starting with the top news/breaking news) in a scrolling format.

The app relies a lot on gestures. Tap and hold over a story and you'll get several options.

The one you will probably use the most is to suggest more / less like this; these two options help Apple News understand what you are into and will over time start to personalize stories based on your preferences.

Typically, "report" in a news app means you find it somehow inappropriate in nature; that's true here, but there are other reasons to report it—such as, it's dated wrong, it's in the wrong category, it's a broken link, or something else.

As you scroll down, you start seeing different categories (Trending Stories in the example below); when you tap the three dots with a circle, you'll get an option to block it, so it won't show in your feed any longer.

When you tap to read a story, there are only a few options. At the top, there's the option to make the text larger or smaller; next to that is the option to share the story with friends (assuming they have Apple News). To get to the next story, there's an option in the lower right corner (or swipe left from the right corner of the screen); to get back to the previous page, tap the back arrow in the upper left corner or swipe right from the left side of the screen.

One criticism of Apple News by some has been its UI; when Apple announced the service along with its partnership with the Los Angeles Times and

Wall Street Journal, many expected a format similar to what you have seen with the magazines section—a full newspaper-type layout.

Worse, many didn't even know how to find the newspaper. And if they did find it, they couldn't search for stories. While the app is pretty resourceful, this is still an early product and some of the features you want might not be there yet.

That said, you can "kind of" read the Los Angeles Times (or any newspaper in Apple News) in a more traditional way. First, find an article in your feed from the publication you want to see more from, and then click the publication's name at the top of the story.

Los Angeles Times

This will bring up the publication along with all the topics from that publication.

If you want to search for a particular story or publication, then swipe from the left of the screen to the right, and search for what you want to find.

Following

At any time, you can swipe from the left edge of the screen to the right and see the channels / topics that you follow.

This is where you are going to be able to look at your history, read saved stories (as noted above), search for stories and publications, and follow or unfollow topics.

To unfollow a category, swipe left over it and select unfollow.

To add a new category, scroll down a little. You'll see suggested topics. Tap the '+' button for any you want to follow.

You can move your categories around by tapping on the Edit button at the top right.

News+

The last section to cover is News+; this is where you'll find all the magazines you love.

The format is similar to the Today screen; magazines you read are at the top; below that are stories pulled from several different magazines that the app thinks you'll be interested in. There's also a more personalized For You section.

When you read articles from the list, it opens in the actual magazine and looks a little different from articles in the Today area.

Anytime you want to read more from a magazine (or see back issues) just click the logo from an article you are reading.

That brings up a list of all the issues you can read as well as some of the latest stories from the magazine.

Tapping the '+' button in the upper right corner will let you follow the publication.

If you long press (press and hold) the magazine cover from your My Magazines section, you can also unfollow, delete, or see back issues from the publication.

To browse all the magazines available, select Browse the Catalog from the main screen (or browse by a category that you are interested in).

This brings up a list of all the magazines you can read (at this writing, there are around 300).

Long press any of them and you can download the magazine, follow it, block it, or browse the back-issue library.

[11]
MAINTAIN AND PROTECT

This chapter will cover:
- Security
- Keychain
- iCloud
- Battery Tips

SECURITY

Passcode (dos and don'ts, tips, etc.)

In this day and age, it's important to keep your device secure. You may or may not want to set up a Touch ID (if it's on your model), but at the very least it's a good idea to maintain a passcode. Anytime your tablet is unlocked, restarted, updated, or erased, it will require a passcode before allowing entry into the tablet. To set up a passcode for your iPad Pro, go to Settings > Passcode, and click on Turn Passcode On. You will be prompted to enter a 4-digit or 6-digit passcode, then re-enter to confirm. Here are a few tips to follow for maximum security:

Do's
   DO create a unique passcode that only you would know
   DO change it every now and then to keep it unknown
   DO select a passcode that can be easily modified later when it's time to change passcodes

Don'ts
   DON'T use a simple passcode like 1234 or 5678
   DON'T use your birthday or birth year
   DON'T use a passcode someone else might have (for example, a shared debit card pin)
   DON'T go right down the middle (2580) or sides (1470 or 3690)

ENCRYPTION

With all of the personal and sensitive information that can be stored on iCloud, security is understandably a very real concern. Apple agrees with this, and protects your data with high level

128-bit AES encryption. Keychain, which you will learn about next, uses 256-bit AES encryption—the same level of encryption used by all of the top banks who need high levels of security for their data. According to Apple, the only things not protected with encryption through iCloud is Mail (because email clients already provide their own security) and iTunes in the Cloud, since music does not contain any personal information.

KEYCHAIN

Have you logged onto a website for the first time in ages and forgotten what kind of password you used? This happens to everyone; some websites require special characters or phrases, while others require small 8-character passwords. iCloud comes with a highly encrypted feature called Keychain that allows you to store passwords and login information in one place. Any of your Apple devices synced with the same iCloud account will be able to load the data from Keychain without any additional steps.

To activate and start using Keychain, simply click on Settings > iCloud and toggle Keychain on, then follow the prompts. After you've added accounts and passwords to Keychain, your Safari browser will automatically fill in fields while you remain logged into iCloud. If you are ready to checkout after doing some online shopping, for example, the credit card information will automatically prefill, so you don't have to enter any sensitive information at all.

iCloud

To really get the full effect of Apple's carefully created ecosystem and be a part of it, you will need to create an iCloud account. Simply put, iCloud is a powerful cloud system that will seamlessly coordinate all of your important devices. The Cloud can be a little difficult to understand, but the best way to think about it is like a storage unit that lives in a secure part of the internet. You are allocated a certain amount of space, and you can put the things that mean the most to you here to keep safe. In the case of iCloud, Apple gives you 5 GB for free.

Your tablet lets you automatically back up certain files such as your photos, mail, contacts, calendars, reminders, and notes. In the event that your tablet is damaged beyond repair or is lost or stolen, your data will still be stored safely on iCloud. To retrieve your information, you can either log onto iCloud.com on a Mac or PC, or log into your iCloud account on another iPad Pro to load the information onto that tablet.

With the introduction of iOS 8 and the iPhone 6 and 6 Plus, Apple rolled out a few major changes. You will now be able to store even more types of documents using iCloud Drive and access them from any smartphone, tablet, or computer. Additionally, up to six family members will now be able to share purchases from iTunes, and the App Store, removing the need to buy an app twice simply because you and a loved one have two different iCloud accounts.

For users who will need more than 5 GB, Apple has dramatically reduced the cost of iCloud:
50 GB is $0.99 per month
200 GB is $2.99 per month
1 TB (1000 GB) is $9.99 per month
2 TB (2000 GB) is $19.99 per month

Battery Tips

The iPad Pro promises amazing battery life. But let's face it, no matter how great the battery is, you probably would love to have just a little bit more life in your charge.

Disable Notifications

My mom told me her battery didn't seem to be lasting very long. I looked at her tablet and could not believe how many notifications were activated. She knows absolutely nothing about stocks, nor does she have any desire to learn, and yet she had stock tickers going. You might want notifications on something like Facebook, but there are probably dozens of notifications running in the background that you don't even know about, nor do you even need to. Getting rid of them is easy; go to Settings, then to Notifications. Anything that shows up as In Notification Center is currently active on your tablet. To disable them, tap on the app and then switch it to off. They aren't gone for good; anytime you want to turn them back on, just go to the very bottom where it says, Not In Notification Center and switch them back on.

Brightness

Turning down the brightness just a shade can do wonders for your tablet and might even give your eyes some needed relief. It's easy to do; go to Settings, then to Brightness. Just move the slider to a setting that you feel comfortable with.

Email

I prefer to know when I get email as soon as it comes. By doing this, my tablet is constantly refreshing email to see if anything has come in; this drains the battery, but not too terribly. If you are the kind of person who doesn't really care when they get email, then it might be good to just switch it from automatic to manual. That way it only checks email when you tap the Mail button. To switch manual on, go to Settings, then to Mail, Contacts, Calendars and finally go to Fetch New Data. Now go to the bottom and tap Manually (you can always switch it back later).

Location, Location, Lo…Battery Hog

Have you heard of location-based apps? These apps use your location to determine where you are exactly. It's actually a great feature if you are using a map of some sort. So, let's say you are looking for somewhere to eat and you have an app that recommends restaurants, it uses your GPS to determine your location, so it can tell what's nearby. That is great for some apps, but it is not so for others. Anytime you use GPS, it's going to drain your battery, so it's a good idea to see what apps are using it and question if you really want them to. Additionally, you can turn it off completely and switch it on only when needed. To do either, go to Settings, then to Location Services, switch any app you don't want to use this service to off (you can always switch it back on later).

Accessorize

90% of you will probably be completely content with these fixes and happy with their battery life; but if you still want more, consider buying a battery pack. Battery packs do make your tablet a bit bulkier (they slide on and attach to the back of your tablet), but they also give you several more hours of life. They cost around $70. Additionally, you can get an external battery charger to slip in your purse or briefcase. These packs let you charge any USB-C device. External battery chargers cost about the same, the one advantage of a charger versus a pack is it will charge any device that has a USB-C, not just the iPad Pro.

The easiest way to save battery life, however, is to go to Settings > Battery and switch on Low Power Mode. This is not the ideal setting for normal tablet use, but if you only have 20% of your battery and need it to last longer, then it's there.

Appendix A: Accessories

Apple Pencil

The biggest companion to the iPad—perhaps the reason you bought the device—is the Apple Pencil. The Pencil looks like a normal stylus, but it's much more sophisticated than that; there's actually a tiny processor inside of it and when you use it, it's scanning for a signal over 240 times a second.

Unlike other styluses, the Apple Pencil has a battery built into it. To charge it, simply connect it to the magnetic side of the iPad. Apple says you can get 30 minutes of life into the Pencil by charging it for just 15 seconds. Don't worry about constantly charging it, however—it will last roughly 12 hours on a full charge.

Using the Apple Pencil is also easy; as soon as you touch the Pencil to your screen, the iPad can sense that it's a Pencil and not a finger. Pressing the Pencil harder on the iPad will make the line or object you are drawing darker; pressing it softer will make it lighter. If you want to add shading, tilt the Pencil; the sensors inside the Pencil calculate the orientation and angle of your hand.

SCRIBBLE FOR APPLE PENCIL

Apple Pencil got a huge upgrade in iPadOS 14 with a new "Scribble feature that lets you use the pencil in search fields—so you can scribble text in a Google search, for example, instead of typing it out.

You can use Scribble anytime there's a text

If you type something wrong, or want to erase it, just put a squiggle line through it.

If you want to highlight a word or sentence, circle it.

You can also connect two words by putting a dash between the words.

Using Apple Pencil With the Notes App

When you use Apple Pencil with the Notes app, Scribble works differently. You are still technically scribbling text, but you are not going to see that instant conversion.

In Notes, Apple Pencil treats the app like a journal, and keeps your handwriting intact.

That's not to say you can turn your scribble into text—the process is just a little different. After you have wrote out the text, tap and highlight it with your finger just like you would any normal text. When the box comes up asking you what to do, select copy as text, and then go to where you want the text to go and paste it.

The Apple Pencil is pretty sophisticated, but if your handwriting is as bad as mine, then there's a bit of a learning curve.

Apple Pencil isn't just for text. It also can also recognize and convert shapes. To use it, draw a shape (i.e. circle, square, etc) as you normally would, and when you get to the end, pause, but don't lift your pencil—just pause. In seconds, it will show a preview of how it thinks the shape should look; if you are satisfied then lift the pencil.

Apple Pencil Settings

Apple Pencil settings are limited. You can access them, but going into the Settings app, and selecting Apple Pencil.

From here there are two settings you should be aware of. The first is "Double Tap"; when you double tap on your Apple Pencil it does something—what it does is decided by you here.

The second thing you should be aware of is Scribble; if you absolutely hate the feature or just need it off for a short period, then tap the toggle switch.

SMART KEYBOARD FOR IPAD PRO

The Keyboard is full-size—meaning it's the same size and spacing you are used to on larger tablets. Being full-size means there's room for shortcuts. Holding down on the CMD button next to the space bar, for example, while you are in Pages, brings up the menu below:

Bold	⌘ B
Italic	⌘ I
Underline	⌘ U
Copy Style	⌘ option C
Add Comment	⌘ shift K
Find	⌘ F
Hide Word Count	⌘ shift W
Hide Ruler	⌘ R
Create Document	⌘ N

If the Keyboard isn't sturdy enough for you, another keyboard to check out is the Logitech Create keyboard; it's about 10 dollars cheaper than the

Apple Keyboard, but works the same way. The Logitech keyboard has a backlight (so you can see the keys in the dark) and charges through the iPad, so there's no need for batteries. It comes at a cost, however—it's about a pound in weight.

APPENDIX B: KEYBOARD SHORTCUTS

The iPad Pro shares one more thing in common with the MacBook: keyboard shortcuts. Because the keyboard has a command key, you'll be able to use the same shortcuts you may already know. Below is a list of them (Note: these shortcuts will not work with every program).

- Command-X – Cuts or removes selected text or item and copies it to the clipboard.
- Command-C – Copies the selected text or item to the clipboard.
- Command-V – Pastes the contents of the clipboard into the document, app, or finder.
- Command-Z – Undoes the previous command.
- Command- Shift-Z – Redoes the previous undo.
- Command-A – Selects all text or items in the running program.

- Command-F – Opens the Find window to find documents or other items.
- Command-G – Finds the next occurrence of a previously found item (i.e. Find Again).
- Command-H – Hides the current running program or front window (Note: this will not work if you have a program running in full screen).
- Command-N – Opens a new document or window.
- Command-O – Opens an item (for instance if you are in Word or Pages and you want to open a previously saved document).
- Command-S – Saves the current document.
- Command-Q – Quits an app.
- Command-Tab – Switches to the next open app (Note: if you don't let go of Command and continue hitting the Tab button, you can continue going to the next app).

Document Shortcuts

The following shortcuts are applicable to supported document software like Word, PowerPoint, Pages, Excel, OpenOffice, etc.

- Command-B – Bold or un-bold the selected text.
- Command-I – Italicize or un-italicize selected text.
- Command-U – Underline or remove underline to selected text.

Appendix C: Welcome to Note Taking 2.0

Note: This is based off Notes for Mac, but the functionality is almost the same.

Why Notes?

If you are new to Apple, then the obvious question on your mind might be: why Notes? What is it good for and when should you use it?

Notes is probably *not* what you want to use to write this year's Christmas Newsletter or create a flier for your lost puppy; Notes really excels when you want to create a shared list, jot down school notes, or do something that doesn't need a lot of formatting.

Notes really shines when you sync it with your iPhone; with your iPhone sync'd, you can write your notes, then use your phone to insert a sketch or image.

Once you have created your Note, you can add it to a folder and everything is searchable, which makes it a very organized way of tracking things.

The Notes Crash Course

To open it, go to the Launchpad icon on your Dock and click the Notes icon.

Notes, like most of the apps in Catalina, syncs to your iPhone and iPad as long as you are logged into the same iCloud account.

Unlike word processing editors that you may be used to, there is no fancy ribbon or menu bar with lots of features. There's a side bar with a list of all your notes (across devices if you use an iPhone / iPad sync'd to your Mac).

On the top is a very basic menu bar.

Views

The first option next to the app resize options (the red / yellow / green dots) is the view toggle.

This toggle switches between a list view of your notes and a thumbnail view (see below).

If you are in list view, then you only need to click the Note one time to open it; if you are in thumbnail view, then you will need to double click it.

Folders

The next button is for creating folders.

This brings up a list of all your folders (if any).

If you don't have one yet, then click New Folder at the bottom of the window.

To rename, delete, or add people to the folder, click the three dots with the circle around them.

Finally, to add a note to a folder, click it from the side, and then drag it into the desired folder.

Once you are done, click the view button again to hide the folders panel.

VIEWING ATTACHMENTS

The next option looks like the button to attach things; that's not correct. It's the option to view all the attachments you have added into notes. When you click on it, you can sort by all the different attachment types (Photos & Videos, Scans, Maps, Websites, Audio, and Documents)

When you double click an attachment, it opens a preview of it (it does *not* open the note which it's found in). If you would like to see the Note that it is in, then right click to bring up the option menu and click "Show in Note."

Delete Note

The next option is pretty straightforward. It deletes the note that you have currently selected.

Creating a Note

Next to the delete button is the "Create a Note" button, which, as you can expect, creates a note. When you open your note, the left panel will have the name of the note with a time stamp, and the right will have an empty text area to write in. The title of the note will change once you start typing text; the first line of text is the title of your note. You cannot rename the title; if you change the first line of text in the note, then the title is changed automatically.

Lock Note

The security on Notes may not seem quite as robust as other word processors, but there is a very resourceful Lock feature that helps keep private notes secure and for your eyes only. To use it, click the Lock icon.

This will bring up a dialog box that asks you to add a password. Now anytime you want to open the Note, you'll need a password. If you forget your password then you will not be able to access your Note, so be careful!

CREATE A TABLE

You can also add Tables to your Note. Personally, I would stick to adding tables into other word processing suites, because this is one feature a bit more cumbersome than other tools out there. But if you want to try it out, click the Tables icon.

This adds a very small table to your note—just two rows and two columns.

To add a row or column, click the three little dots on top of the column or to the left of the row, then click what you want to add. You can also delete it using this method.

CREATE A CHECKLIST

If you are using Notes to create a shared list between people (or just a list for yourself), click the Check icon.

This turns each line of text into a list. Hitting return on your keyboard will create a new list item; hitting return twice will take it out of list mode and return it to normal typing.

○ Bullet One
○ Bullet Two

You can click inside any of the circles and check an item off. If you made a mistake, then just uncheck it again.

○ Bullet One
⊘ Bullet Two

You can also move a list item up or down by right clicking it, then going to "Move List Item."

By right clicking, you can also go to More and check off all items (or uncheck all items).

ADD A STYLE

While you can't do as much to the format as you could in other word processors, Notes does have basic styles. To access them, click the Aa icon.

This gives you a drop-down of all the possible styles available.

ADDING SKETCHES AND IMAGES

One of the many areas Apple has always really shined is with syncing between devices. Using Notes for Mac with your iPhone, you can add in sketches or take photos.

To get started, go to the photos icon. This brings down a drop down of all your options. You can, of course, add any photo on your Mac with the Photos option.

Using the next three options (Take Photo, Scan Documents, Add Sketch) will bring up an image that asks you to connect to your phone to complete the tasks (make sure you are on the same network).

When you add a sketch, you draw it on your phone.

Once you hit done on your phone, it will automatically appear in Notes for Mac.

Adding Collaborators

If you want to add others to your note, click the icon with the person and +.

Next click "Note 'New Note'".

It will ask how you want to add them. Through messages, a link, AirDrop, etc.

When you're ready, click share, but before you do, click the Permissions drop-down and make sure it's set up the way you want. You can either let the note be view-only for others or you can let them make changes.

Sharing Notes

If you want to share the note without adding the person to the note, click the share icon.

Next, pick how you would like to share the note.

Searching Notes

The last option on the toolbar is the search box. This lets you search all of your notes for different keywords. For example, whenever I go somewhere with a public Wi-Fi, I add the network key to a Wi-Fi password note (I don't recommend this for sensitive passwords); whenever I need to quickly find it, I search for "WiFi" and it comes up immediately.

Exporting Notes

Now that we've seen all the features on the toolbar, let's go up one level to the top menu bar. Everything you did in the toolbar, you can also do there; there are also, however, a few extra features.

The first is exporting a Note as a PDF. That's found under File > Export as PDF.

Above Export is the Import option; personally, I find it easier just to share a note from another device, but if you have a copy somewhere and have a reason to import it, then you would go here.

Pinning Notes

Pinning notes is a very basic, but useful feature; when you click on a note and then select to Pin it from File > Pin Note, it sticks it at the top of all your notes to make it easier to find.

![File menu screenshot showing options: New Note ⌘N, New Folder ⇧⌘N, Add People To..., Close ⌘W, Import from iPhone, Import to Notes..., Export as PDF..., Share, Unpin Note, Lock Note, Print... ⌘P]

Attaching Files

Unlike many word processing apps, you can actually attach files to Notes. Go to Edit > Attach File.

Spell Check

Like any word processing software, there is a spell checker buried in the top menu. You can start spell check by going to Edit > Spelling and Grammar. By default, it checks spelling / grammar as you type.

Font Formatter

Finally, while changing the font color / type is not quite as simple as Pages or Word, it is still possible. Go to Format > Font.

iPhone Notes

Now that you know your way around Notes, let's look at how it works on the iPad (which is almost identical to how it looks on the iPhone).

In terms of functionality, everything is almost exactly the same. The difference is just where things are located.

At first glance, Notes looks basically the same as it always has. Notice that little plus sign above the keyboard? That's what's different.

Tap the '+' button one time, and you'll see the options that have been added.

Starting from the left side is a checkmark, which is what you press if you'd like to make a checklist instead of a note. For each new checkmark, just tap the return button on the keyboard.

The 'Aa' button is what you would press if you would like to format the note a little (larger fonts, bold, bulleted text, etc.).

Formatting

Title

Heading

Body ✓

• Bulleted List

– Dashed List

The little camera button will let you add a photo you have taken, or let you take a photo from within the app and insert it.

Photo Library

Take Photo or Video

Cancel

And finally, the squiggly line lets you draw in the Notes app; when you press it, you'll see three different brushes (pen, marker, and pencil) which each work a little differently, as well as a ruler and eraser. This is really the biggest difference in Notes in iOS; unlike the Mac, Notes in iOS lets you draw on your screen—something you can do on your Mac only by syncing to your iPhone or iPad.

There's also a round black circle—tapping that lets you change the color of the brush.

Just tap the Done button in the upper right corner once you've picked your color and it will be changed.

Once you tap the Done button after you've finished drawing, you will go back to the note. If you tap the drawing, however, it will activate it again and you can make changes or add to your drawing.

○ Check list
○ Item 2
○ Item 3

Hello

It's obviously not the most advance drawing app—but that's the point—it's not supposed to be. As the name of the app says, this app is just for jotting or drawing quick notes.

In the Settings menu a Search option has been added at the top. There are a lot of Settings in iOS and there are more and more with each update—Search Settings let you quickly access the setting you want. So, for instance, if you want to stop getting notifications for a certain app, you no longer have to thumb through endless apps—now just search for it.

Settings

Q Search Settings

Airplane Mode

Notes has also been added to Safari, so if you want to add a website to a note, it's now possible.

Whenever you see the option to use Markup you will be using the Notes interface.

Appendix: Shortcut Keys

General Shortcuts

Create a new note	Command-N
Create a new folder	Shift-Command-N
Show the main Notes window	Command-0 (zero)
Show notes in a list	Command-1
Show notes in gallery view	Command-2
Search all notes	Option-Command-F
Print a note	Command-P

Edit Shortcuts

Attach a file	Shift-Command-A
Create a link	Command-K
Insert a table	Option-Command-T
Apply Title format	Shift-Command-T
Apply Heading format	Shift-Command-H
Apply Subheading format	Shift-Command-J
Apply Body format	Shift-Command-B
Apply Checklist format	Shift-Command-L
Increase font size	Command-Plus sign
Decrease font size	Command-Minus sign
Increase list level	Command-] or Tab
Decrease list level	Command-[or Shift-Tab
Mark or unmark a checklist item	Shift-Command-U

INDEX

A

Accessibility 112
Adding / Removing Contacts .61, 85, 113, 116, 118, 190
AirDrop 58, 77
AirPlay 43, 44, 45, 47, 132
AirPods 148
App Store ... 70, 84, 91, 93, 94, 117, 118, 129, 142, 172, 189
Apple Arcade 144
Apple Card 144
Apple Key 17, 19, 200
Apple Music .84, 92, 144, 157, 158, 160, 163, 166, 168, 170
Apple News 144, 171, 172, 173, 174, 175, 176, 179
Apple Pencil 10, 17, 19, 20, 23, 24, 44, 193, 194, 195, 196, 197, 198
Apple TV+ 144

B

Battery 185, 189, 191, 192
Bluetooth 15
Bookmarks 87
Brightness 109, 113, 190
Buying Apps 92

C

Calendar ... 11, 84, 85, 95, 116
Camera 124, 125, 127, 131
Control Center 29, 30, 31, 37, 111

D

Dictation 54
Do Not Disturb . 109, 110, 111
Dock 59

E

Email 90, 190
Emoji 55

F

Facebook ... 86, 109, 116, 117, 189
FaceTime 60, 61, 82
Family Sharing.. 109, 118, 119
Files App 147, 153
Find My 84, 102, 103, 118, 148
Flashlight 29

G

Gestures 10, 27, 50

H

Handoff 109, 123
Hide Photos 134
Home Button 12

I

iCloud 50, 88, 95, 96, 103, 112, 118, 144, 145, 146, 147, 148, 149, 150, 152, 156, 185, 186, 187, 188, 189
iMessage 28, 58, 61, 65, 66, 68, 70, 71, 119, 137
iMessage App 70
Installing / Removing Apps . 70
iTunes 84, 91, 92, 118, 158, 187, 189
iTunes Match 158

K

Keyboard 19, 55, 56, 199, 201
Keyboard Shortcuts 201
Keychain 185, 187

L

Live Photos 131

M

Mail 90, 190
Maps 11, 26, 84, 96, 97, 98, 99, 100, 101
Memoji 26
Multitask 28, 37

N

Notes 11, 25, 84, 103, 104, 106, 108, 196
Notifications 30, 37, 58, 76, 109, 111, 189, 190

O

Organizing Apps 62

P

Panoramic Photo 126
Phone Calls 27, 60
Photo Album 134
Photo Albums ... 130, 132, 134
Portrait Photo 127, 128
Privacy 114, 116

R

Reading Lists 87, 89
Reminders 11

S

Safari 10, 28, 51, 62, 85, 88, 90, 108, 116, 123, 187
Safari Tabs 88, 90
Security 115, 185
Sidecar 11, 39, 43, 46, 47
Siri .. 11, 27, 99, 140, 141, 142, 143, 171
Smart Keyboard 199
Software Updates 24, 94
Sounds 109, 113
Split View 81
Stacks 35
Stocks 111

T

Text Messages 26, 65, 74, 121
TV 43, 91, 132, 158
Twitter 86, 109, 117

U

USB-C .. 13, 14, 15, 17, 21, 191
Users & Groups 127

V

Video 124

W

Walking 52
Wallpaper 109, 113
Widgets ... 24, 25, 34, 37, 109, 111
WiFi 44, 60, 123

About the Author

Scott La Counte is a librarian and writer. His first book, *Quiet, Please: Dispatches from a Public Librarian* (Da Capo 2008) was the editor's choice for the Chicago Tribune and a Discovery title for the Los Angeles Times; in 2011, he published the YA book The N00b Warriors, which became a #1 Amazon bestseller; his most recent book is *#OrganicJesus: Finding Your Way to an Unprocessed, GMO-Free Christianity* (Kregel 2016).

He has written dozens of best-selling how-to guides on tech products.

You can connect with him at ScottDouglas.org.